HOLD ON TO WHAT IS GOOD

HOLD ON TO WHAT IS GOOD

A Dementia Caregiver's Story and a Memorial to an Exceptional Being

PHYLLIS M. BROOKS

Taliloquay Publishing

Taliloquay Publishing/Phyllis M. Brooks
Wendell, Massachusetts
phyllismichalbrooks.com
taliloquay.com

First Printing, 2024
ISBN 979-8-218-35777-1

Dedicated in love to

Mark Charles Stewart II

October 17, 1949-June 7, 2023

Contents

Preface

This is not a "how to" book on living with dementia or caring for a person with dementia. It is a recording of my journey through the unspeakable with widely varying degrees of acceptance and grace. Each person has to navigate such a journey by themself. This is also a tribute to my partner Mark, to his life and his spirit. It is a love poem of memory, respect, pain and joy.

The title, *Hold On to What Is Good,* is the first line of a Pueblo poem (English version) that inspired me to write a song about my experience living with a person with dementia. It became the "theme song" of the dementia caregiver's group I met with online once a week during the last two years of Mark's illness. No one who has not experienced living with and caring for a person with dementia can understand what we go through. The group was a lifeline for me. We could express emotions that we couldn't anywhere else, knowing that these people would understand completely and without judgment. I salute my fellow caregivers, those brave, loving people who persist, day after day, living moment by stressful moment, working to fend off as long as possible the ultimate destination of their loved one.

But then, death is the ultimate destination for us all as human beings. Some of us may go quietly and peacefully, others fight for every last breath, every last experience. Mark was one of the latter, and I travelled with him as best I could to the end.

The chapters in this book alternate between my experience as a caregiver and vignettes from Mark's life story. Much of the descriptions of my daily life as a caregiver are from pieces I submitted to my writing group during this time. We would choose a word, phrase or theme for each session. The rest is from my journal, which I kept during the last few years of my caretaking experience.

Mark's life narrative is in his own words for the most part, since I was recording some of his experiences before he changed. There is much of his life that had to be left out. My hope is that his spirit comes through in what I was able to include. Enjoy the narrative of the life of an exceptional loving and light-filled being, lending poignance to his last few years.

Hold on to what is good
Hold on to what is good
Even if it's just a smile
Even if it's just a smile
Even if it's only once in a while.

Hold on to what is good
Hold on to what is good
Even if it's just a touch
Even if it's just a touch
Even if it's not very much.

Hold on to what is good
Hold on to what is good
Even if it's just a laugh returned
Even if it's just a laugh returned
A shadow of joy that's soon unlearned.

Hold on to what is good
Hold on to what is good
Even if it's just a spark
Even if it's just a spark
A spark in the eyes that soon goes dark.
Hold on
Hold on
Hold on
Phyllis Brooks - August 28, 2022

I

The Worst Day of My Life?

Phyllis' Journal

My life partner Mark begins to develop dementia in 2016. At least that is when it starts to be obvious. I am away when Mark becomes very sick from two tick bites. By the time I reach home, he is having trouble talking. Medication doesn't seem to help much. Mark does his best to continue being himself, but he can no longer hold down jobs. He had been doing small building projects, mostly renovating or repairing homes. Mark's memory seems affected as well as his speech. And understandably he becomes moody.

By the next year, Mark's condition is deteriorating, but I still can leave him by himself, or so I believe. Our finances are veering toward desperate, so I find a part-time job at minimum wage.

During this time our wood stove becomes inoperable. The chimney has not been properly cleaned for a couple of years, though I didn't know this. The interior of the chimney is broken. When I consult a chimney expert, he says that creosote has been seeping through to the outside of the chimney, and it would be dangerous to start a fire in the stove even with a new liner, because it could burn down the house.

We are now without heat. It's March, still very cold here in New England. We have to use small electric heaters to keep the pipes (and us) from freezing. We find an organization that will supply us with a propane heater if we can find a propane supplier who will carry us. This proves difficult. Mark had become a hoarder. Our yard looks like a junk yard. This is putting off all the propane companies I contact. So I set about trying to clear up the yard enough to achieve a contract with one. Later in the year Mark's daughter will come for a few days to help and will do a great job. But that March we are still without heat.

I can't leave Mark by himself with no heat while I go to work, so I drop him off at our local co-op. I leave him with magazines and money for snacks. These are things he can still manage. I meet him for lunch and tell him I will be back for him around 5.

At work at the end of the day I am told I am no longer needed, and that today would be my last day. No advance warning. They are downsizing in order to hire an office manager. I am just a file clerk. So I leave that night wondering how I am going to support Mark and myself. It had been a long time since he could cope with a job.

When I arrive at the co-op to pick him up, Mark isn't where I had left him. I ask around, but no one remembers seeing him leave. I walk around the nearby streets looking for him. He has my cell phone, so I use the phone at the co-op to try to reach him, but apparently the phone is either turned off or he can't manage to work it. I go to the local hospital to check if anyone had been admitted with his name or description. I also check with the police department. Then I run into a friend who lets me use her cell phone. I phone home to our land line. He answers. Apparently a friend of his had seen him at the co-op and offered him a ride home, so he took it.

Around three hours after I had started to look for him, I head home. Emotionally I am what I call *on the edge*. I'd lost my job. I had wanted to be with Mark just for comfort, whatever he could supply in his current condition, but I hadn't been able to find him. I'd become frantic with worry about him being lost somewhere. Although glad to discover he is okay, now I know I can no longer leave him by himself away from home. And we still don't have heat. I guess it's a good thing I'd been let go from the job, since I would have had to leave anyway.

Eventually I am able to enroll Mark for Supplemental Security Income (SSI) payments, which double our income from my Social Security of $750/month. Most of his goes towards food and his clothes and some medications. Around real-estate tax time I have to dip into my meager savings to pay. We are keeping our heads above water, barely.

We still don't have heat until the day before Thanksgiving, when a decent propane company agrees to take us on. We'd been without real heat for four cold months, two in the spring and two in the fall. Our last electric bill was astronomical. Again I dip into my meager savings. I am grateful to the organization that supplies us with a propane stove and the compassionate oil company that finally agrees to keep our tank filled.

That day in March is probably the worst day of my life—until then. There is more to come.

2

Pre-Birth

Mark's Story

When you are born you do not usually remember the details of your plans for that lifetime; they reveal themselves at the proper time to be useful. I know that I incarnated on Earth this time because Earth had need of the level of light I was able to bring. I was not the only one to do this; there were and are millions of these volunteers. I am just one of them.

A lifetime spreads before you as lines of energy. There are many possible paths. If life were totally planned out beforehand, what would be the use of it? It is an adventure, to be lived moment to moment. I have heard that the theme of this Cosmic Day is "Courage". This helps to make at least some sense of the chaos, pain, and barbarity that I knew I was incarnating into.

I had memories of other lifetimes, and the pain and cruelty that had been inflicted on me, and that sometimes I had inflicted as well on others. I knew it was not an easy assignment. Every now and then I am reminded that one of the things I am here to do is to offer help to the "hard cases". Still, you do make contracts with others in the setting that you will find yourself after third-dimensional birth on Earth. My parents did not live up to their contracts. It happens.

My grandparents were my salvation. They were from an ancient line of Scottish Druids, connected with the invisible realms and the Akashic Record. My grandmother especially was to be my guide and mentor when my father failed to protect me from my mother's physical and psychic abuse. Of course looking back, I see what I learned and how my experiences have not only colored my life, but also made me aware in certain ways that I might not have been aware, and taught me things that I perhaps might not have learned otherwise. All is experience.

<h1 style="text-align:center">3</h1>

Why Not?

Phyllis' Journal

Why not let Mark drive solo to the hardware store? It's early days still. March of 2018, and he has been driving okay, with me as copilot. I'm still used to the Mark I've known so long. He has been to the hardware store so many times on his own, what could go wrong? But he doesn't return by nightfall. I call my son to come help search, and we notify the Orange police.

We find him in the parking lot of Walmart. The hardware store was closed by the time he got there. He has filled the car with bags of tangelos from Walmart. He is smiling and offering the policemen oranges. They confiscate his license. At least I do not have to be the one to take away his license. I feel like an idiot for letting him go driving by himself. It's hard to realize, hard to *accept* how much he has changed and how much he can no longer do.

Why not leave my glasses on the table when I run upstairs to do some work on the computer? Because they may not be there when I come back. I may find them in a day or two. Mark likes to tuck things away in places I often can't imagine. Until then I'll just have to wear the old ones, the ones I got twenty years ago.

Why not let him go outside to walk in the woods, on the land? He's always been an outdoor person. Of course, he may go walking on our dirt road, and a guy he knows may stop to ask if he wants a ride, and an hour or so later that guy is at my door telling me he dropped Mark off in the next town over and left him there.

"Don't you know he has dementia?"

"Well, yes, I'd heard that. I went back to pick him up after I was done, but he wasn't there and I couldn't find him. Thought you'd like to know. Oh, and he has my gloves."

An hour or so later, after driving the streets of Orange, I give up and dial 911. Mark's last encounter with police was not friendly, so I left that for last. Yes, he was picked up and taken to the Athol hospital. I find him there, full of needles and monitors. He seems calm, even happy. He says, as best he can, that he wanted to see people. I think that's what he means. They were being very nice to him.

Of course, I can't keep him inside and I can't ride herd on him every minute. I just try to keep him on our land. Our interactions with others are limited by Covid. Our yoga classes have stopped. Both of us are lonely.

I hope that I never forget how Mark used to be. His laughter and the sparkle in his eyes. How he would confidently tackle anything that needed to be done, fixed, whatever. How we used to laugh together. How connected he was to multidimensionality, to "spirit" if you will.

Now I don't know who will wake up next to me in the morning. Often he seems to be mostly in some other world. He needs help showering, putting on his clothes, taking vitamin pills. He angers easily. When he is clean and dressed and fed, I breathe a sigh of relief that it all got done without mishap or a "blow up" in rage. I know that the beautiful person I lived with and loved for over twenty years is in there somewhere. I see glimpses now and then. I hope I never forget him.

4

My Birth

Mark's Story

I remember being in my mother, floating. But I knew I was separate from her. Emotionally she was one way, I was another. When they induced labor with some kind of shot, I didn't want to come out, so they decided to do a cesarean. I remember swimming around, and then suddenly there was light, more than I had ever seen. But I was still in partial darkness.

The doctor (his name was Dr. Clark) pulled me out into the light, and I started screaming my head off, because the bright lights hurt so much. I continued screaming while they washed me, and then they put me into this box that also had bright lights. I kept screaming, I don't know for how long. I thought that if I kept screaming, they'd come and put me into a dark place. I wanted out of here!

A woman appeared in my head. I mean, I saw her though my

eyes were closed to the bright white light. She was an African lady, clearly a spirit being.

She said to me, "Hush little one! If you don't stop crying, we won't be able to keep you in your body!" The sheer enormity of her appearance stifled my next scream. This was maybe because she asked me to, but more likely because I no longer felt alone.

Later I wished I had kept screaming long enough to separate my spirit from my body, but I found out I had volunteered to be here, on this planet at this crucial time to help in its liberation, me and millions of others, and I would be here as long as needed.

Why did I often regret my decision to stay here? My mother. She did not want me. I learned later that my mother had been trying to get rid of me. She had multiple sclerosis, and her doctor was afraid that this pregnancy would harm her, so at five months I was an abortion that failed. I knew that it hadn't actually failed; the baby that had originally grown in her womb had passed on, and I slipped into the body. I was a "walk-in" from the start. I was aware from the very beginning. All was as it was supposed to be.

I weighed three pounds two ounces at birth. After the first week I went down to two pounds three ounces. I fit perfectly in my dad's hand. I was in an incubator for four and a half months—the youngest and smallest baby to survive up until then in that hospital. I stayed in that incubator with the bright lights and very little human contact. I know now that it was fortunate that I did not bond with my mother, so that later when she hurt me it did not harm me as deeply as it could have.

Occasionally in my dreams I would find myself in a universe of light. This was not the glaring blinding light of the premie ward, but a soft light that enveloped me in what I can only call love. I would know nothing about love if it weren't for my multidimensional friends and my grandparents.

Mark and his sister Polly

5

A Day in the Life

Phyllis' Journal

I hear Mark start to get up during the night. Why not just roll over and go back to sleep? He's been pretty good lately at going to the bathroom on his own. But sometimes he forgets where the bathroom is, especially in the fog of just waking up, and I really don't want to clean up a large puddle of man-pee, that's if I can find where he left it this time. So I get up and escort him to the bathroom at 3 AM.

Sometimes he leaves bed in the middle of the night and wanders around, moving stuff and shouting about having to do something that he can't do, shouting at people only he can see. I can't understand what he's saying. I just try to go back to sleep and leave him to it. He won't listen to me anyway when he's in this mood. I'll just fix what's fixable in the morning.

It's 5 AM. He decides it's time to rise. Usually he's up at first light, unless he's been up all night. I help him, since often he has trouble sitting up due to shoulder pains. He's off to the bathroom. I follow.

"Time for a shower," I tell him. I've learned not to ask if he wants a shower, just to let him know it's the thing to do right now. I help him undress (he usually sleeps in his clothes) and lather him with soap, then lead him into the shower stall to rinse off. Most days he seems to enjoy the hot water.

"Uh, uh, uh!" He's ready to leave the shower. I towel him dry, massaging his back and rubbing linament into his shoulders. Then I help him into a shirt, jeans, socks, pants and shoes. In the winter there's a first layer of long underwear.

Why not leave him to dress himself as I start breakfast? Oh dear. He's put his boots on, without first putting on his pants. Now we have to take off the boots and start over.

I serve him his oatmeal. Being Scots he has to have it every day. It's tradition. Besides, he once told me that the reason it took invaders so long to capture Scotland was because the invaders ate too much meat and were always constipated. So it's oatmeal every morning, liberally laced with fruit. He sits and stares at it awhile. I know that he will start eating eventually and I leave him to it as I start the washer, to make sure he has clean clothes tomorrow.

I walk into the living room. Crunch! "What the hell?!" I shout. I'm standing on crystals spread out all over the floor. Mark has been into creating patterns, mandalas with anything to hand, mostly quartz crystals. But anything will do—bottle caps, quarters, drill bits. Usually these creations are on tables or the kitchen counter or sometimes the bed. It keeps him happy, so I just ignore or admire them.

But *Crunch!* It just slipped out. "What the hell?!"

6

Diablo to the Rescue

Mark's Story

We had a chihuahua named Diablo, who ran on a wire outside. My dad decided when I was around three years old that he couldn't trust me to stay in the yard, so he put a harness on me and attached me to another wire like Diablo's. The first time he put me on it I sat down and cried until he brought me in. I told him I didn't like it. So he decided to make me a fenced-in play yard. It was about twelve feet by eighteen feet with a sandbox in it. I used to play there and was fairly happy.

A neighbor girl from across the street who was my age was used to running free. She laughed at me because I was in a cage. I felt bad about this. I told her to help me out so we could play together. She told me she couldn't play with me, because her dad was a doctor and made more money than my dad. She wouldn't help me out. Then she left me alone.

I looked at Diablo, who was now attached by a chain to a pipe railing in the cement stairs. He was digging a hole in the ground to lie in, to keep cool. This gave me the idea to dig a hole under the fence. After digging my way out, I felt free!

One of our neighbors had a duplex, part of which was rented to a family who owned a German Shepherd. I wanted to visit the kids who lived on the other side from the dog. I had to cross a neighbor's yard. While I was in the middle of that yard, the German Shepherd smelled me. He jumped over the hedge and started stalking me. I knew he was going to bite me. I turned and ran, and fell on my face. I started screaming.

Little Diablo *broke his chain* and jumped over the bushes into the neighbor's yard. This tiny chihuahua stood between me and the German Shepherd, growling ferociously.

The Shepherd cocked his head, and gave him a look that said, "You've got to be kidding! I'm going to eat you!" Diablo feinted to one side, then dashed between the other dog's legs to jump up and bite his balls. Then he ran back to guard me again. He was very quick.

The Shepherd looked at him, clearly thinking, "You didn't really do that! You couldn't possibly do that again!" Diablo feinted in a different direction, ran between the dog's front legs this time, and jumped up and bit his balls—again! And came back to guard me. The Shepherd still held his ground, but he was looking a bit doubtful about continuing to tangle with Diablo. At this point Diablo lunged after the Shepherd, who turned and fled back to his own yard, with this little chihuahua nipping at his heels. It was very funny!

Diablo then ran to our *front* yard and started barking, to alert my mom that something was wrong. Diablo should have been on a chain in the *back* yard, so he knew that barking from the front of the house would attract attention. Thank you, you smart, brave dog! I began to feel that there were unseen beings looking out for me.

Mark's parents with Diablo.

7

The Lost "and Thens"

Phyllis' Journal

My writing group has chosen the prompt "and then". I realize that our lives are a series of "and thens". We live in a third-dimensional world subject to linear time moving through space. We're also told by metaphysicians of old and physicists today that this is all illusion. There is only the now. So this series of "this happened and then this happened and then this" *ad infinitum* is merely a stretching out of the present moment, in order to examine all that is happening, our emotions and actions, supposedly simultaneously. It's hard, if not impossible, to consciously wrap a third dimensional mind around this multidimensional concept. We just do it.

Cause and effect is a concept of the third dimension. We call it karma or the golden rule. What I do to you I do to myself. I'm told that it's an immutable law in our universe, so that we remember, eventually, that we are all One. All of our stories depend on "and then". Our concepts of ourselves depend on these stories. It's a box we live in, until we don't. We need to break down the individual moments into a line, a timeline, to begin to understand who we are and how our thoughts and actions affect ourselves and those around us. This is the normal human experience in our third-dimensional world.

It's hard to navigate the third dimension without a concept of time. Mark has lost his "and thens". When I try to tell him how to do something, I have to break it down into steps, and then only give him one step at a time. If I tell him more than one step, he becomes confused and frustrated. In our box of time and space, we need our "and thens" in order to function.

Mark tends to be attracted to what is right in front of him. Words are often too abstract. He is easily distracted by objects in his field of vision. He no longer can conceive beyond this moment. He can no longer relate cause to effect. Yet his conscious mind still resides in the third dimension, in a third-dimensional body, where this is necessary. One step at a time he can usually manage. I can't lay out the whole schedule of events or steps when giving him instructions, such as when he tries to help me in the kitchen. He has to finish cutting up the carrots before I tell him to put them in the pot. He has to focus on one step at a time. I have to tell him to put on his pants before he put on his shoes. He can no longer see that the other way around just won't work.

I learn to rewind what is happening, constantly. What day it is. What we are doing and plan to do that day. I need to repeat these many times, *never* saying "I just told you that!"

I REACH OUT

I reach out to Mark
when he is scared or anxious.
"You are safe. You are loved."
I've heard it said
that all pain stems from
feeling separate, feeling alone.
But when he is in
a paranoid head space
he rejects all contact.
He cannot connect.
How alone he must feel!

Phyllis Brooks
February 6, 2022

8

My Druidic Education: Becoming Aware of Frequencies

Mark's Story

When I was three years old I started spending time with my grandparents. I doubt I would still be alive if it weren't for my father's parents. My grandmother came from Newfoundland, one of twelve sisters and one brother, from fisher folk. She was sent to live with a sister in Boston for a chance at a better life. My grandfather was the youngest of a family of twelve brothers and one sister. His older brother had married one of my grandmother's sisters. Gramp had grown up on a potato farm on Prince Edward Island. Being the youngest, he had to take off on his own to make a life for himself, so he went to live with a brother in Boston. There he met my grandmother. They recognized each other and married.

Both were from unbroken lines of Scottish Druids. My grandfather could work with any animal; his tie with the Nature kingdom was innate. My grandmother was in a direct line of the priestesses of the divine feminine of old, and she knew energetically how to use that. Neither of them was formally educated. Their ability to perceive had not been tampered with or hampered by formal education. They had lived many lifetimes together. I once asked Gramp how his gardens always flourished even when everyone else's turned brown. He said, "I just give the plants what they tell me to give them." Simple.

They tried to impart Druidic wisdom to their only son, my father, but he wanted nothing to do with spiritual teachings. I however was an eager sponge, soaking up everything they had to offer. They were of Nature. They knew they were eternal beings temporarily inhabiting physical bodies. They taught me I was energy. Their teachings made sense to me, as the world around me didn't.

My grandparents each had talents, and they had forged a relationship of equality, humor, and mutual respect. They were not without faults, however. My grandfather had a temper. He usually woke at first light, around 4:30 AM and ate some oatmeal before going out to do chores until breakfast at 8. My grandmother would make his oatmeal and leave it out for him.

One night when I was staying over at their place, I heard them arguing. My grandfather shouted, "Because I said so! So there!" in a very disrespectful way. My grandmother just smiled to herself and went to bed.

The next morning I heard him go into the kitchen. "ARGHHH!"

he screamed. A dish hit the wall, breaking, and silver went crashing all over, bouncing off the floor. My grandmother was chuckling.

I asked her, "What's going on?" She said, "I had to teach him a lesson. The Dead Sea has less salt in it than his oatmeal today!" She had put salt in the sugar bowl. He was nicer to her later. I learned that being harsh often comes with paybacks.

When I was three, my grandmother started teaching me. She wanted me to know that there was more to life than what I might learn in school, so she started showing me that everything had a name. That name was generally different from what people called it. She showed me how to tell the difference between the name that scholars called a plant or a rock or whatever, and its true name, the name that this form of being thought of itself. She taught me that everything has a consciousness and a true name.

Inside that true name, each one is different as well as the same. Every single thing has its own frequency, down to atoms and molecules and up to planets, galaxies and beyond, onto infinity in both directions.

These are not so much words as energetic signatures. Almost always the energy behind the words that scholars have developed for things are different from their true energy, the name each being knows itself as. The energetic signature is, in fact, the frequency with which a being is attached to the Prime Creator. All the beings within a group are a fiber in the trunk-sound-vibration of the collective whole of that group. There's the overall vibration of the group, and then each part has its own variation that helps to make up the whole.

This is hard to put into words, easier to just feel. The smallness and the largeness are the same. Everything is made up of energy. The energy holds everything together. So everything is different and the same, unique as well as part of the Whole. The "glue" that holds it all together is love, love without conditions.

My grandmother's ability to teach me came from my guidance system through her. She was "reading" my higher self. The teachings she gave my sister were very different from those she gave me. My sister had her own skills, but they were different from mine.

These exercises helped me later in life to be able to communicate with people who needed help dealing with their emotions. One time I witnessed an incipient fight between two bikers. One whipped out a knife. I was able to align my vibrations with his and go up to him and take away the knife, diffusing the situation. My grandmother's lessons were invaluable to me.

9

Two Points of View

Phyllis' Journal

Here are a few scenarios during our day. Mark's thoughts are in italics. I'm sure I don't do him justice, trying to read his mind, but I do my best.

M: *Light. Get up. Have to pee...She's gone! "Uh Uh Uh!" Oh there she is.*
P: "Good morning, Mark!"
M: *Morning. That's it. Pee.*

P: "Time for a shower!"
M: *What's that? Oh yeah that way.*

M: *Shoes there. Put them on.*
P: "Mark, you have to put your pants on before your shoes. Or you won't be able to put them on. they won't fit. Here..."
M: *Huh? Shoes are right there. Pants are all the way over there. Oh well.*

–––––––

(Mark is busy lining up crystals on the table)

P: "Time for breakfast! We need to clear off the table so we can eat." *(P starts picking up crystals to move them)*

M: *Humph*

–––––––

P: "I have a meeting online. I'll be busy upstairs for about an hour."

M: *(ten minutes later, a voice from outside)* "Hellloooo! Is anybody there?"

–––––––

M: *There's something wrong there. That thing on the floor needs to be fixed. (kneels)*

P: "Mark, I'm making dinner. I can't do it if you're pulling the rug from under my feet."

M: *It has to be right. What's she on about now? It needs fixing. (continues to straighten the rug)*

–––––––

M: "I have nothing! I have nothing! I have nothing!"

P: "You have food, clothes, a house! I'm here for you. I love you!"

M: "I have nothing!" *(He begins to cry).* "Agggghhhh!"

–––––––

P: "Mark, my potholders are missing. Do you know where they are? I need them."

M: *What's she on about now? How should I know? What's a potholder?* "I didn't do it!"

–––––––

M: *Those bare spots need covering. I'll put this stuff there.*

P: "Mark, please don't put straw on top of the places where I've already planted seeds! They won't grow."

M: *What's she mean? Okay I'll clean up these places.*

P: "Mark, please leave the straw in the garden around the plants.

We need it there to stop weeds from growing. It isn't useful in the woodshed."

M: *Huh? What's she mean? I'll just nod as if I know and keep going.*

P: "Please hand me a spoon?...No, that's a fork. ...no that's a screwdriver. Never mind."

M: *What's wrong with me? I can't do it! I'm fucked!*

P: Mark, please take your shoes off before getting into bed.
M: *What? Why? Oh okay. (takes off shoes)*
P: "And your belt. And your pants."
M: *No way.. Sleep now. (crawls into bed)*
P: "Oh well. Choose my battles. (Sigh) "Good night, Love"
M: "Love you."

10

My Druidic Education:
Learning From Nature

Mark's Story

My grandmother started showing me different herbs in the woods and fields around the house when I was around four years old. We would go out and gather herbs to dry or to make into tinctures and decoctions, depending on the plant and/or the intended use. One day she had me go out to pick hops. There were nine clumps of hops growing up the side of a building. I went and harvested what I thought was the right amount for making a sleeping draught. This was actually for me, because I was so hyper I had trouble sleeping. I tried the medicine that night, and it worked.

The next day she had me do it again, but this time I was to go ask, "Which plants want to come and make medicine to help me sleep?" When I heard, "Yes," I picked from those plants only. We

31

made medicine from this harvest. They were knock-out drops! The first medicine, if I drank enough, would put me to sleep. With the second medicine, a few drops in a cup of water would *immediately* put me to sleep.

Everything is sentient, and because it's sentient we always have to ask about everything. When you receive an "Okay, we're going to work together," it's 100 percent. It's kind of like with a human, when you force someone to do something that they don't want to, versus when they are willing to. Plants and chemicals have those same properties.

So if a person collects an herb to make a tea, when the plant is first asked and says "yes", the tea is more potent by far. It has the heart. That's the key. When the heart says "yes", you've got all of it together. All of the plant's lineage is tied up with what you're making—millions and billions of connections, years, experience. There's a power that comes in as you make things in this cooperative, co-creative way.

When you reach all the way back through this lineage, by asking first, the result really is way more potent than if you just go and take from the plant. When the "yes" is happening, it changes everything. The "yes" itself opens doors that if you don't have open, the power is much less. Some power is there, but it's nothing compared to what's available when you have full cooperation.

Mark's grandmother with Diablo.

11

Going Beyond

Phyllis' Journal

Occasionally the loving, gentle, kind Mark I knew surfaces. More often lately it's the angry Mark, and that's hard. He can't live by himself. I don't want to leave him, no matter his mental state. I remember him as he was; we share a deep love. I also have to acknowledge him as he is. He often says, "I love you!" He often curses me. I work at dealing with my own emotions at these times. I work at learning patience. I do feel compassion. I still and always will have love for this incredible being who helped save me from two toxic relationships and helped me start to access my multi-dimensional connection to my true Self. He helped me to feel what a true love relationship could be.

GOING BEYOND

Often on my life path
I hit a brick wall.
An energetic blockage
I need to go beyond
All I know, all I think,
All I ever did before.
Going beyond
Letting go
Of the past
Burdens of old experiences
Of the illusion of separation
Interpreted as pain.
Letting go of programs
Telling me I'm not good enough
That I cannot
Of weariness that moans
"I will not."
Breaking through
Letting go
The bricks dissolve
As I align with
A higher version
Of my Self.
Phyllis Brooks / November 13, 2022

12

My Druidic Education: Communicating With Spirits

Mark's Story

My grandmother also taught me to speak with beings that had no body, those we call spirits or ghosts. There was a sailor who had lived in their house since he died in 1889. He was a sea captain. He had things to teach me energetically about life on the ocean. My grandmother helped me interface myself so I could receive pictures in my mind of some of his experiences. She changed the frequency of my being to match his, in order to do this. She never violated my personality, but she guided me by coming into my being and showing me how to alter my frequency, so that I could communicate with these spirits. When you match frequency with another, you are separate, but there's no boundaries stopping energetic conversation. So energetically you now experience each other without interference and without harm to either.

I could tell when I meshed with the captain that he wasn't happy. I asked Gram why he didn't go where he could be happy. She told me that that was between him and the Creator. I thought it was all great fun!

When I got to be four, it was easier to walk around, so we would go walking in the woods. Almost everywhere we went, there were spirits of those who had come before us, the Red People. They were comfortable with themselves as they were. I noticed that was different than with the sea captain. My grandmother then told me that there was another level to life that had to do with opening one's heart to the ocean of love without conditions. The sea captain had been a nice man, but he didn't understand love without conditions. The Red People were so enmeshed in the lovingness of Nature that they were entirely comfortable. Having or not having a body was all the same to them.

These spirits would inhabit certain places that they felt tied to by choice. In their mind's eye, eternity is a long time, so staying in a place for a few hundred or thousand years is nothing. Eventually they would move on.

My grandmother taught me how, as with the captain, to mesh myself with each one of them, if I chose. When I could allow myself to mesh with all of the beings, all of the living plants, all of the insects, all of the microbes, all of the rock beings, then I would feel a special kind of peacefulness and sense of belonging, a knowing that I was not alone.

My grandmother helped me by partially giving me direction and helping me change my body frequency in order to experience these things. She told me that at some point she was not going to be there to help me, and that I had to learn to do for myself what she was now doing for me. She had made it seem so easy that I couldn't see any reason why she couldn't keep doing it. I asked her why I needed to learn to do it myself. She told me that all the things we had done were merely a beginning of what I would do, and that I had to make up my own mind how to balance myself, without help.

I told her that I didn't think I was capable of doing all this myself. She looked at me and shook her head. "Well, we'll have to figure it out," she replied. I know now that she was being kind and firm at the same time. She could see that I didn't have enough self-confidence to venture out on my own and do things that I had no support for from the greater world.

13

❦

Drifting Away

Phyllis' Journal

Living with Mark I try to keep up my spirits. Often he will pick up my feelings and mirror them back to me, so it's best to stay as calm and as "happy" as possible. It's hard watching him deteriorate. It's extra hard when he goes into a rage (remembering his childhood?) or becomes paranoid. Then I become the enemy (his mother?).

"Where are my tools?!"
"Where's my wallet? You took it!"

I must have bought him at least 3 wallets. He keeps hiding and then losing them. At first I give him money to put in the wallets. After a while I give him less and less, since he seems determined to hide them (and forget where). I often find a wallet sandwiched between layers of jeans in his closet or stuck into the toe of an old boot. I never do find them all.

Mark loves quartz crystals and has a large collection of them. He makes mandalas all over the house (later using anything to hand, not just crystals). I sometimes reach into my coat pocket and find a crystal or two that he has stashed there. Once I find a heart-shaped pink stone stuffed into my purse, which makes me smile. He can be so sweet at times and then later go into a rage. This is the hardest part for me. I had heard people say similar things about living with an alcoholic or drug addict, that their moods would change abruptly. Sometimes I feel like a battered wife, though he never touches me physically. The battering is psychological, and all the worse because I can't really blame him for it or leave him. He truly can't help what is happening in his brain.

Every other week in my online writing group we choose a "prompt" and then write about it and share with each other. I write a few songs and poems from these prompts. This brings out my deepest feelings in a way that nothing else can. Sometimes I just go into the woods and scream or cry when he is being mean. Sometimes his just saying, "I love you" will bring me to tears. Here's one song that best expresses my feelings about my life now with Mark.

WHERE DID YOU GO MY FRIEND?

Where did you go my friend?
Where did you go my love?
Where did you go, and how can I find you
You've gone where I cannot go.

What do you think my friend?

How do you feel my love?
What goes on behind those vacant eyes
How can I follow your mind?

When seldom you speak my friend
Words are all jumbled up--
A puzzle, a maze, an alphabet craze--
You know what you mean but I don't.

You live in a different world
That I have no passport to;
I only hope that you have found friends there
So you don't feel alone as I do.

Sometimes you shout hateful things,
My mind knows it's not your fault,
But I start to wonder if I ever knew you
I work to keep open my heart

.

Sometimes we share a hug
Our hearts in synch for a beat;
Then I remember how it once was,
Hold on to this moment—hold on...

Where did you go my friend?
Where did you go my love?
You never said goodbye, you just drifted away;
You've gone where I cannot go,
You've gone where I cannot go.

Phyllis Brooks / September 18, 2022

I4

❧

My Druidic Education: Love Without Conditions

Mark's Story

Gramp had a collection of antique watches which was his pride and joy. Each was handmade. He must have had around seventeen of them that he had been collecting.

I was seven years old at the time. They left to go to town. I went into Gramp's room and opened all the watches. Some of the gears looked of similar sizes. I took them all apart and piled the like-size gears together. I believed that I could put the watches all back together again, but of course I couldn't. It would have been a real job for an expert watch maker. My grandfather came home. He'd spent his whole life collecting these watches, and he was not a rich man. These gold watches were something he could sell for his retirement. I had ruined them.

I apologized to him, but it was way too little, too late. I shouldn't have touched them. Gramp was a passionate man, and very strong. In the house where we lived there was a hole in the kitchen wall. Gramp had asked my dad (in his younger years) to do something. My dad had said, "No, and so what?!" and walked out of the house. The hole in the wall extended through the horsehair plaster, through the wooden lathes, through the one inch boards on the outside of the wall, through the one inch clapboards. Gramp made it in order to punch my dad as he went by, after sassing him.

So my grandfather was standing over his ruined watch collection, as my grandmother admonished, "Don't kill him. He doesn't know what he did." Gramp hadn't breathed for at least two minutes as he gazed at the pile of watch parts. When she said that, he let out one huge breath. I ran up and gave him a hug. He said, "I love you, and get away from me for a while." For two or three days it was hard for him to speak to me.

In the end we loved each other as before. They really taught me love without conditions.

Mark's grandfather

15

Rage and Consequences

Phyllis' Journal

"You took my tools! You stole my wallet! I hate you! I want to kill you!" It's very hard when the person you love most in the world shouts things like this at you. My head knows that he can't help it, he doesn't really mean it, but it still hurts.

To release the anguish, the pain of love lost I have to go out to the shelter of the woods and sob, as I allow the energy of the trees to calm me. Sometimes I think he confuses me with his mother, and I can understand the rage better. But the stress is still there. I am under stress day and night. I doubt I have had a full night's sleep in years.

I call his daughter in Maine to see if she can come down and help for a weekend or so, but she is busy with her life. I understand that. This is my life. I feel frazzled, on the edge of sanity at times.

I would love to leave, even for one night, but I can't see how to do that. When I have tried bringing someone in to watch him for a few hours, he has objected and thrown them out. He can be pretty scary when he is angry. Even I become frightened at times. I *know* he will never hurt me. After what his mother did to him, Mark doesn't believe in hitting anyone. But is that still true?

One day as I am washing dishes, Mark comes up behind me and grabs my shoulders. "Where are my tools? What have you done with them?" He shakes me a bit. Some young guys have stolen quite a few of his tools. Also he has left some of his tools at the last place he worked, and I don't know where that is. The man he was working for called and left a phone message, "Mark come pick up your tools." But this man didn't leave a name or number, and we didn't have that service on our phone, so I can't go retrieve them. Mark, of course, doesn't remember where or who it is.

So I turn around and tell him, "Let go of me!" He does, but he is still angry. I need someone to talk to. I call his daughter in Maine. She is scared for me and wants to call the police. I tell her, "NO! Don't do that. I just needed someone to talk to! He'll be okay now."

He calms down. We are both working outside in the garden. It's hot. I go in the house for a drink of water. A big policeman comes barging into the house. He looks startled to see me. He asks me what happened. I told him everything is okay. Apparently Mark's daughter tried to call us, but since we were outside we couldn't answer. She panicked and called the Massachusetts state police to go round and check on us. A law in Massachusetts says that the "abused party" can't refuse to charge someone who has "attacked" them.

I tell him it wasn't an attack. Mark has dementia and was angry and confused. He is okay now. But there were already cops outside who had grabbed Mark in the garden, tied him up, put him into a van and taken him off to jail. So the cop in the house with me decides he has to make the arrest legitimate and refuses to believe me that nothing harmful has happened.

I have to go to the police station and wait six hours, because they won't release Mark to me. His daughter has to drive down from Maine to get him released, and then it is to a hospital emergency waiting room until a bed opens up in a psych unit in another hospital. He is assigned a week of supervision there.

The hospital is an hour's drive from home. I have to go in each day to bring him food he will eat and try to calm him down. On arrival they want to give him high blood pressure medication, but he never had high blood pressure before. He was just terrified by the treatment he had undergone, being strapped down to a gurney for the ride to the hospital. He didn't understand what was happening or why. It was torture for a person with dementia. After four days they release him, because they don't know what to do with him. He just keeps pacing up and down the hall.

I wish his daughter had believed me when I told her not to call the police, that they would only make things worse. I'm just glad he went peacefully with them, so he wasn't shot. His shoulders never recover from being tied above his head in the van. His shoulders were already painful as a result of his construction work.

Thus we are consigned to around nine months of court appearances and a stint with a court-appointed psychiatrist to make sure that Mark isn't "faking" dementia. This experience makes me leery of talking to anyone about what is going on with me and Mark.

I despair at being able to share my feelings with anyone, in case they will react by calling authorities to "help" me. I resist talking with friends and stuff my feelings deep inside. Of course they don't stay there.

Mark and I become under surveillance by an organization called LifePath after our last court appearance.. This is the only useful thing to come out of our experience with the judicial system. LifePath has many excellent programs for seniors. It's where I find the dementia caregivers Zoom group that helps me so much. Finally I can recount my experiences and express my feelings to people who will understand and not panic or judge! Just being heard is such a relief and so healing!

16

⁓

Abuse

Mark's Story

The main reason that I had no self-confidence was the way I was being treated by my parents, especially my mother. She was highly educated. She spoke six languages (English, French, Spanish, Russian, Mandarin Chinese, and Latin), and could write in three of them. She was an accomplished track star. My mother, a girl from the North, had been awarded a track and physics scholarship to the University of South Carolina. This was during the depression and was quite a feat. One part of her family had "come over on the Mayflower", which made her feel even more special.

My mother met my dad at a sorority function and they hit it off right away, in a physical way. She became pregnant with my sister (who is 11 years older than me). Becoming pregnant in the late 1930's, my mother was forced to marry and drop out of college. Her family were Presbyterians and did not like my dad's family. They felt that my dad and his family were socially beneath them. When my sister was born, my mother was diagnosed with multiple sclerosis.

She became increasingly bitter towards my dad. By the time I came along, if my dad said something was black, she'd say it was white. The raw hatred they felt towards each other was like a mill-stone around my and my sister's necks, for we felt they held us to blame for their situation. I learned to have a very thick skin about what other people thought of me and my role in their life. If I hadn't felt that way, I would have committed suicide early on.

The other side to my mother's personality was that she had to control absolutely every facet of our lives. I was more of a free spirit than my sister, and even Polly gave both my parents gray hair in her teen years, when she would ride on the back of motorcycles and smoke cigarettes. My sister was very good to me, though, often attempting to save me from my mother when Mom was on the rampage. And me? I was simply trying to be whatever I needed to be in each moment.

My mother didn't know how to open her heart. She was mentally tortured by the beliefs and teachings of the very strict "Christian" family she was born to. She was shattered and she didn't know how to love. Also she felt frustrated at having her life plans so disrupted by pregnancy and forced marriage.

There's a darkness and a light here. In all of my earthly life-times, I have always acted from my heart to the best of my ability at the time, and I would learn from my mistakes. So living with my mother, a person who didn't know how to open her heart, was traumatic. Because of her experience of growing up without love, she did not know how to love with her heart. She wasn't able to be a loving human, let alone a mother.

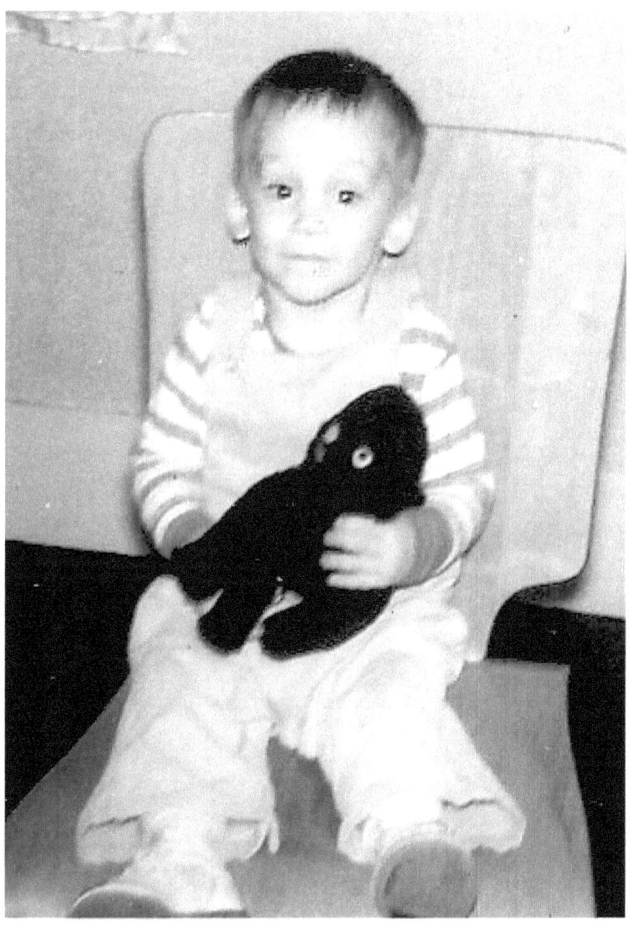

She used to beat me with a leather belt until my legs were black and blue and bloody. Her treatment of me was the reason I so often stayed with my grandparents.

It was my fourth birthday. Dad had bought me a kite and was helping me put it together. Being me, I was trying to help him but didn't know what I was doing. I broke one of the crossbeams. After we'd taped it together and whipped it to make it stronger, I thought that I could ask him for help.

I said, "Dad, I know I do some things wrong, and for those things you might need to punish me. But could you stop Mom from beating me, just because she feels like it?"

Dad told me that he couldn't help me. I got the feeling that he was more than a little afraid of her. I then knew that I was entirely on my own. I had to figure out how to protect myself.

17

A Walk in the Woods

Phyllis' Journal

It's early April. The sun is shining on a rare day of relatively mild temperatures here in western Massachusetts. Mark and I go for a walk through the woods behind our house, farther than I usually venture. We are enveloped by the scent of pine and hemlock, which are beginning to awaken. Mark directs us towards the sound of rushing waters. The stream must be just ahead. We go up a small hill and look down at the stream, swollen by spring snow melt. Mark points upstream. We see a small waterfall, another farther up, and another beyond that. It's wonderful how Mark knows these woods and all the lovely places. We have a short peaceful interlude of beauty shared together, and both of us begin to relax.

Mark has always been an outdoor person. He needs Nature to feel whole. This is why I cannot see consigning him to an institution, even when his behavior becomes untenable. I will hold out as long as I can.

This is becoming more problematic. In February I schedule an online interview with a spiritual counselor. Mark is very obstreperous during it, yelling and stomping around in the background. I become emotional. I had hoped the counselor could shed some light on why this was happening. I'd been taught that we create our reality, we are responsible for it. How are we are creating this?

The counselor only says, "You are not a victim. You are not responsible for Mark. You need to take care of yourself."

How can I abandon Mark to some short-staffed nursing home where he will be pumped full of drugs? How can I abandon him when he has helped me so much in the past? How can I abandon my love?

The counselor tells me to shut my eyes and envision myself in the future. I see a bright white light. That's all. It feels encouraging though, even if it means death!

As the interview continues, my emotions flood out. I can't stop crying. My heart hurts when Mark becomes unreachable. How much pain and fear I must be holding to have my emotions bubble up so uncontrollably. I feel stuck, helpless. I don't know what to do. This is what is behind my uncontrollable emotional outburst.

Some tips from dementia counselors on how to communicate:

- use eye contact
- one thing at a time

- don't argue
- respond to feelings, not facts
- redirect and distract

What if he won't look at me? What if he is too loud to hear me? What if he won't let me hug, or even touch him? Staying calm is my most important lesson and often still the hardest.

When Mark is trying to tell me something I can't understand, he starts jumping up and down and screaming. If I say, "I know it's frustrating to not be able to say what you want," he often winds down and stops. Then I try to figure out what he is trying to tell me. Sometimes he just forgets and goes about his business doing something else. If I have not understood what he was saying, I can allow myself to feel like a failure and get upset, or I can realize I have done my best and just vow to try again another time.

I learned in the sound-healing workshops I attended throughout the 1980s that crying, even screaming, can be a great release for inner tension, AS LONG AS I REMEMBER TO BREATHE DEEPLY while I am emoting. Gulping down the sobs only leads them to fester within. Breathing deeply allows the energies to be released, and usually I feel lighter afterwards.

our woods

18

Formal Education

Mark's Story

By the time I started school, I was in total rebellion. I had to deal with the unfairness of my mom's treatment and my anger, so I started doing strange things in school that I knew were wrong. I remember I used to pee on the radiator in the boy's bathroom, filling the place with the smell of urine. I felt that if I was going to get beaten for things I couldn't help, I might as well do something really bad. The beatings would happen anyway, so who cares?

In first grade the other children were learning to read. I looked at the primer, which was about "Dick, Jane, Sally and Spot." I compared that to my grandmother's teachings. Two things happened. First, I didn't want to learn to read that; it was not worth my time. Second, my streak of rebellion came out and I said to myself, "If I don't read, I won't have to do homework." The beatings fractured my being. I decided to teach myself to read secretly, while pretending in school that I couldn't read. This caused me more beatings at home, for being a dumb stupid kid.

I never passed a test, until it came to a multiple choice intelligence test. This was very simple. The test showed that I had a high I.Q. At six or seven I was not sophisticated enough to know to lie on the tests. I did better than anyone else in the class. I just put marks in the boxes and got 97 percent right. They couldn't figure it out. The teacher treated me as if I was incredibly intelligent but just couldn't do the work. So she passed me. In the parent-teacher meetings, my parents were told that the teachers couldn't understand how I couldn't read but had passed this test unbelievably, while failing all the other tests I was given. I was a very sweet child to all the teachers.

At the same time, I was developing a whole different personality, and it was exciting. I was going to teach myself to read, while pretending not to read! This was the first time that I was actually doing something on my own. It felt good to take charge of at least a part of my life.

My rebellion also took a new form. I started walking to school a different way than I had been told to. I took different side streets where there was no police or safety patrol help to cross the streets. I would run through back yards and poke around in peoples' garages, where they had interesting things like old antique cars. I was practicing being the worst kid I could imagine and enjoying it. It helped me deal with my sense of unfairness at my treatment by those that should have loved me.

Meanwhile my grandmother was continuing my other education. She started showing me different herbs in the woods and fields around the house. In Nature I learned to feel love and connectedness.

I was then pretending not to read, and I was being mischievous to my fellow students, while being nice to my teachers. But I couldn't deny, though I tried, that I knew how to listen and be with Nature. Instead of me manipulating the situation, I got what I wanted from Nature by asking with an open heart, and Nature replied. There is no need to use cunning and intellect to lie to receive what you want with Nature. I could no longer deny that human interaction was part of Nature. This was the beginning of my conscious growth. I decided then that I needed to clean up every part of my life, as it came up. This teaching showed me that I could interface with any being perfectly, as I chose.

I now felt that I didn't want to go to school, I didn't want to live with my parents, and that I could make it on my own in the world. I was six. I packed a change of clothes in a kerchief and was ready to leave. My grandfather sat me down and said, "The world is not set up for someone your age to live alone. You could make your own way, and find food, but you also need to clothe yourself and have money. A person your age cannot work for money. If you try to, you would be arrested and sent to a foster home, and we would be unable to see you."

I realized that there were things that I didn't know that were beyond my control. I decided to go back to my parents and figure out how to get along with them. I felt more in control now. My parents were like squabbling children. If I could contact beings and change my frequency, I could hold my lovingness in such a way that they couldn't damage me. So I went home.

Mark and his sister Polly

19

Going Walkabout

Phyllis' Journal

Mark always prefers being outdoors, no matter the weather. Even as his mental capacities deteriorate, this does not change. He "works" in the garden, though I often have to fix things there later. Sometimes he will weed the wrong plants. He loves picking the small green tomatoes and squash, and bringing them proudly to me. When I set up our watering system for the year, he goes out and "fixes" it, undoing everything I had done. I don't have the heart to try again. I just let him water with the hose everyday. It helps keep him busy.

After his trip to Orange, that had ended up in the hospital, Mark starts to just take off down the road. I try to keep an eye on him, but he is good at evading scrutiny, whether on purpose or not. One time he is halfway to the Wendell Country Store, which is around four miles away, before I catch up with him. He seems ready to enter the car. Other times he doesn't want to go back with me.

Another time I need to drive to the post office to pick up our mail, and of course he comes with me. I leave the car to go into the post office. Sometimes he would just stay in the car, other times he would follow me in. This time I finish quickly. He hadn't followed me. I don't see him around the car or in the store next door. Then I catch a glimpse of him way down the road. I try to follow, but he disappears. Around the place he seemed to disappear I see a long driveway. There are a few houses along it. All around are woods.

Finally, at the end of that road I see a woman in her yard. Yes, she'd seen him, and she points which way he has gone. I follow, bushwacking through the woods, calling his name. After a while I see him coming towards me. I am so relieved to find him that I can't be upset with him. We walk back to the car together. I guess he has had enough adventure for the day, as he comes willingly.

One night after dinner he goes out for a few minutes. When I have finished cleaning up, I go out to check on him. It's after dark. He is gone. I drive towards the center of town and finally catch up to him. Luckily he hasn't gone the other way. He has begun to take off more and more. I begin to keep notes on his disappearances, looking for a pattern that might help curb them.

January 18, 2022: Mark goes walkabout while I am at the dentist. I had told him where I was going and left numerous notes around the house, but he got scared and felt abandoned. He was picked up by police who were there when I arrive home. The local police are very nice and understanding, so different from the state police previously.

January 22: Mark goes walkabout and is brought back by some friendly neighbors.

January 24: I order an ID bracelet for him and talk with LifePath about his roaming.

January 25: A LifePath representative comes here, suggests hiring sitters. When I'd tried that in the past he had thrown a tantrum and thrown them out. It seems I'm the only one he permits to take care of him.

January 29: Mark goes out at night. I have to drive around looking for him. I call the police.

February 20: The ID bracelet arrives. Mark doesn't seem to mind wearing it, luckily. Mark is restless and determined to go out. I offer to take him shopping to the co-op. I go to retrieve my car keys. He is not waiting for me at the car. I drive after him. He is on his way down the hill towards the next town over. Later I wonder if he thought he was going to the hardware store for building supplies? I stop to pick him up, but he won't enter the car. He turns around and starts towards the Country Store. I follow a while. I want to call the police for help, but my cell phone doesn't work in most of Wendell, so I have to turn back and use the land line at the house.

By the time both I and the police arrive at the Country Store, someone has already picked him up there and driven him down the hill to the depot. Wendell people are so accommodating! The Orange police are alerted. He is found halfway on his way to Orange, quite a trek. He must have been walking fast. They bring him back. He seems okay by then, no longer claiming I am out to kill him, as he had been doing.

March 31: I'm at my Zoom support group. Afterwards Mark has

disappeared. The cashier at the Country Store phones to say that Mark is there. I go pick him up. He is laughing, happy. He tells me he "took a wrong turn" and ended up there. He had found one of his wallets (lost for months) with money in it. So he went to the Country Store to buy a drink. He is feeling normal again; it lifts his spirits to be able to walk into a store and buy something. I go along with his mood; it's great! But it hurts my heart to understand how broken he feels most of the time, how disconnected from ordinary life.

There's an organization in our town called Village Neighbors. Through them I am able to contact a very nice man, Stephen, who had volunteered to accompany elderly people on walks. He starts to come over once a week, right around the time that Mark seems to become restless and want to take off. I hope this will keep him from going walkabout. It does seem to help. But he won't go on long walks unless I go along with them. He gets anxious when I'm not around.

Eventually, after about a year, Mark seems to be slowing down during these walks. He begins to start the dementia shuffle. It doesn't stop him, but it does slow him down, and there are no more walkabouts.

20

She's In My Head!

Mark's Story

I had been getting along better with my mother, since my change of heart through my experiences with the Nature kingdom. It was in October, near to my birthday. I was reading *Journey to the Center of the Earth* under my bedcovers, with a flashlight. My mother came into my room to drop off some clean laundry. I was very still, but she saw the light. She pulled the covers off and saw what I was reading. She believed I had been lying to her about everything. She started up the beatings again. This of course re-instigated my rebellion. She screamed at me that I was ruining the family name because I pretended to be stupid, and nobody else in the family was dumb. As soon as I knew what she wanted me to do, I would try to do the opposite. This only increased her fury.

Around this time, my dad got sent away on business. I was downstairs in the basement, where we hung clothes to dry near the

65

furnace. Mom told me not to go near the furnace, because it would burn me. I went over to the furnace and pretended to touch it. She lost it. She came over and grabbed my hands and held them on the furnace until they melted and stuck to the furnace.

By the time my sister came home, mom had realized she'd done something way wrong, and she was putting burn ointment and bandages on my hands. My sister didn't believe my mom's story for a minute, that I had done it to myself. They had words.

The next morning, before I left for school, my mother begged me not to say anything to the people at school about what had happened. If I did, I would probably be put in a foster home, she warned. I went to school and the teacher asked what had happened to me. I got scared. It was the first time in my life I felt really scared. Even when my mom burned my hands I was too busy dealing with the pain to be scared. But now I was shaking. I felt something in the back of my mind. It was as if my mom was psychically trying to control what I said.

I didn't know how to answer the teacher, so I told her I fell down on the blacktop and skinned my hands. She didn't believe me. She sent me to the nurse to make sure my hands were okay. The nurse took off the bandages and said, "It looks as if your hands have been burned." I denied it. There was a conference with my mom. She said that I just fell down. The school nurse told me, "If you're having trouble at home, you can come and talk to us, and we will find you another place to be."

During this time I was walking home different ways than I was supposed to. I went into a garage that had a home-made hot rod made from a 1930's model A. I don't know what possessed me to do this, but I decided to put dirt in the gas tank. I guess I was just acting out my anger. This car was what the kid drove to high school in, and it was his pride and joy.

A few weeks later, I walked through his yard and went into the garage again. This time he was watching and caught me. He accused me of putting dirt in his gas tank, but I denied it. He got my name and went to my parents and the school. The whole story came out. I was forbidden to walk to school any way but the prescribed way.

I started walking home every day the way I was told to. I felt a little tickle at the base of my head, just above my top vertebra, at the base of my brain. It wasn't me. It was an invasion of my personal space. It was just like when the teacher asked me how I'd hurt my hands, and I felt that my mom was trying to make me not talk about it. I didn't say anything to my mom when I got home, but I thought to myself, "I have to check this out."

The next day I got out of school and ran over a way I wasn't supposed to go. I made sure no one was watching me. My mother beat the crap out of me when I got home, for not walking home the right way. I had felt the tickle in the back of my brain on the way home.

"That's what it is! She's inside my head!" I told myself. I knew this was what was happening. That's how she knew all kinds of things about me that she had told me, "mothers just know". The next day I walked home the way I was supposed to, but I pictured in my mind the way I had gone the day before. When I felt the tickle in my head, I took a sheet of golden light and slammed it against the place she was entering my mind. It sealed her out completely!

When I got home, she just about killed me. But she never came into my mind again. I didn't know where I'd gotten the idea of that golden light, but now I know I'd gotten it from the Akashic Record, the same as the answers to the IQ test.

The school now knew that I could read, so I had to do the homework. I didn't do very well that year, but I did manage to earn C's.

21

Life Goes On

Phyllis' Journal

By January of 2022 we're now in the sixth year of Mark's mental decline. I have to accept that he is not going to get better. The days all blend into each other. Often I have to concentrate to figure out what day it is. I eat when I'm hungry and make something for Mark when he seems to need it. We must keep his blood sugar up! We no longer can have a real schedule. Maybe he sleeps until noon one day and then is up another at 5:30 AM or even 2 or 3.

Things are accomplished. He has showers, I help him put on clean clothes. We go shopping for socks, boots, food. But there is no fixed schedule, no set time for this or that. I usually follow his lead, noting clues as to what he needs at the moment. The days all blend into each other.

Lately I often find myself experiencing mind fog. I have to stop to remember where I'm going, what I'm doing. "They" say that caretakers of people with dementia have a greater chance of developing dementia themselves, which is scary. But I can understand. Living under constant stress, the back and forth of "I love you!" and "I hate you!", never a full night's sleep, constantly interrupted to deal with a crisis or need makes it so that any project is accomplished piecemeal, if at all. When my writing group decides on the prompt "the unexpected". This song comes to me.

THE UNEXPECTED
Life goes on day to day
Nothing ever changes
Leading a humdrum existence
Waiting for the unexpected.

News on the radio's all the same
As the day before
Just plug in different names and places
All is going to hell.

Can't see much of a future
The tunnel ahead seems dark
Just one foot in front of the other
A circular path
Repeating the past
Yearning for the unexpected.

I know that change begins with me
I wonder what I can do.
Spiritual leaders say "Just be.
Be Love, it'll come right soon."

Waiting for the unexpected
Yearning for the unexpected
Looking for the path to take me there
To be the unexpected
To live life unexpected
To live life unexpected.
(Be careful what you wish for!)

Phyllis Brooks / September 23, 2022

22

I've Got to Get Out
Of Here!

Mark's Story

As I started sixth grade, I was becoming more and more de-
pressed. I seemed happy, but underneath was a deep feeling, a
knowing that I did not sign up for this. There was something terribly wrong with me. I was four feet nine inches tall and weighed one
hundred forty pounds. Everything was going okay on the surface.
My teacher liked me. He was hard on me, but he liked me, and I felt
good about him. The first few weeks went okay.

It was just before Kennedy was elected president. Something
was going on in my psyche. I was unable to pull myself back. I was
meshing almost entirely with the greater whole that was American
business: might is right, kindness is weakness, hopefulness is fool-
ish. No matter how much I walked in the woods, I couldn't free

myself. I didn't realize I was tapping into a collective consciousness of darkness. I thought it was me. The meshing I had learned from my grandmother and the Nature beings was always loving. No one had told me that the darkness was something that could be tuned into in the same way. I didn't know that I could be separate from the things that I tuned into. The Nature beings are love without condition. I didn't know that I could pull back from the darkness.

Between my 11th birthday in mid-October and the end of the month, I gradually decided that I didn't want to be on the planet any more. I knew my guidance system would stop me from taking my own life. So the day before election day, I decided I would cross the street and throw myself in front of a car. There's different levels in my mind. Some are completely private. I was careful to use only the private places in my brain to plan this.

When I saw a car coming, I crossed the street. I held the thought of throwing myself in front of the car in the private part of my brain, until the car was only fifteen feet away. Then I threw myself in front of it. I couldn't fall! I should have been killed, but my mother was watching and managed to catch me with her mental energy, and she moved me enough to ensure I was only injured very badly. My temple hit the door handle of the car, instead of me landing in front of it as I had wanted.

There was a huge bright flash of light. I found out later that the impact had flipped me backwards, so that I hit the back of my head on a stone wall. By the time I got to the hospital, I had lost almost half the blood in my body. I needed a massive transfusion. When I became conscious again, I was floating above my body in the hospital.

I decided that my body was battered, and seeing as how I wanted out of here, I went towards the pink light. I was told as I approached this golden place, "You cannot come here now." So I flew back to float over my body. People came and went. My body was not awake.

I stayed there for what seemed a long time, although I had no sense of time. Later I found out it was nine days. Somewhere around the fifth day two doctors came in, looking at my chart.

One said to the other, "Do you think he'll ever wake up?" The other replied, "Nah, and if he does, he'll be a vegetable."

I got scared. I still don't know how I could become scared without a body to feel fear. I decided that now they would *have* to let me enter the golden place, if I was going to be a vegetable otherwise, so I went there. But as I got close, the voice again told me that I couldn't come in. It was not my time yet, I would have to go back. I still had things to do on earth.

When my dad came in the next day, he asked the doctor, "What's wrong with him?" The doctor said, "We don't know. He's perfectly sound, he's just not awake. It's as if he doesn't want to come back."

The next day my dad told me, "Charlie, I don't know if you can hear me. There's things you like to do in this life. You like to hunt, to fish, you like to be in the outdoors. You can't do any of that without a body." He kept talking during the whole visiting hour. Then he got up and went away.

I thought all night about what he had said. The next morning I decided I wanted a body. So I re-entered my body. Something happened, something different from anything before in my lifetime.

I came into my body and I was perfectly aligned. This new perfect alignment was possible because my guidance team worked on me non-stop while I was out of body. Being a walk-in, I had not directed the formation of this body in the womb. That was done by the soul who later left during the abortion. Many of the things that were associated with the genetic line of that body were now removed out of my way. Not all of it, but the ties were cut, so I could pick and choose what I wanted. When I was finally back in my body, I felt I had at last come home. Before that, every step I took, every move I made, was in part foreign to me.

I woke up and they released me two days later. My overall body light quotient was ten times what it was before I got hit by the car. By the time I was twelve, I was coordinated and playing sports. It was as if I had had a total body makeover.

The makeover agent was my friend and major multidimensional spiritual councilor, Broken Arrow. He had been my brother in five Native American lifetimes. We would run through the woods together. Our bodies then were perfect for running, moving and feeling all the plants and animals around us. When I came back into my body in the hospital, I had a sense of the holiness of all of creation. I found out later that Broken Arrow is an aspect of Thoth, as well as the Keeper of the Kiva of the Hopi.

23

Merely Experiencing

Phyllis' Journal

March 4, 2022: I am taking the laundry out of the washer, putting it into a basket to hang up around the house to dry. Something unknown triggers Mark. Suddenly he grabs an armload of the wet laundry and sets off towards the door, without his coat. It's very cold out. I try to stop him, put my hand on his arm. He pulls back and pushes me against the wall. I fall and bruise my hip and arm. Mark is wild and angry. "I have nothing." I let him go, I have no choice. He is bigger than I am and still strong.

I call the local police to help me find him (though I don't mention the push). Outside I find the wet clothes Mark had grabbed strewn around the yard. I drive down to the end of our road. Mark is there but refuses to enter the car. A local policeman shows up. He is very kind. We give Mark a choice, go with the policeman or with me? Mark finally decides to go with me. When we reach home, he hops out of the car and starts off, but I warn him he will have to go with the policeman if he decamps again. He comes back to the house reluctantly, eventually calms down and is okay the rest of the day, but he is up all night moving stuff around.

March 5: Mark seems very confused. He sets off before breakfast without a coat. I refuse to follow this time until I have eaten something. I find him on his way back, around a half hour later. He is cold and confused.

March 6: Mark is very belligerent, not wanting me to help him but not able to do things by himself. He wants to go out. He is yelling, wants out of the house. So I take him food shopping.

March 16-18: Mark was In a rage yesterday. Today he is really messed up. It's scary. At my dementia support group everyone expresses grief around how their person yells and treats them. I am not alone.

I am starting to notice how tense my body is all the time. A friend took a photo of me recently and I saw my shoulders were hunched up. I hadn't realized. When sitting still I am never really still; my foot is moving or hand or some part of my body. I can't seem to sit still; I am non-stop jittery.

A passage in Neil Donald Walsh's *Conversations With God* caught my attention years ago, before Mark and I entered the shadowy realms of dementia. I printed it out and stuck it on my bathroom mirror as a constant reminder.

The reason that the true master does not complain
is that the true master is not suffering
but simply experiencing a set of circumstances
that you would call insufferable.
Neil Donald Walsh, *Conversations With God*

Often in the past when events around me seemed overwhelming I would repeat over and over, "I'm merely experiencing! I'm merely experiencing!" It would help. I would feel more empowered, One time I was driving in the middle lane of a three lane highway when my car just quit on me at a red light. I started to panic. Then I remembered, "I'm merely experiencing! I'm merely experiencing!" Immediately a tow truck pulled up behind me. I hopped out of my car and ran over to ask him for assistance. He took me to a nearby gas station, where I found out that a major part of my motor needed replacing, and they were able to do it. Such scenarios have happened to and around me often.

A commentator I follow online recently states that whenever he complains to his spiritual guides about the difficult times he is going through, they always exclaim, "What a wonderful opportunity!"

When I remember to apply these concepts to my current situation it can help. Often I find this difficult. My thoughts don't seem to affect *what* is happening, only how I respond to it. Reminding myself that I am "merely experiencing" and to take advantage of this "marvelous opportunity" can calm me enough to be able to accept help.

When I wonder how I am ever going to manage Mark while driving an hour to his neurology appointment in a place I have never been before, some friends offer to drive us. They do not live nearby, so it means a lot of traveling for them. They come to pick us up, navigate our way to the mega-hospital complex and help us find the right building and the right office. Then they wait a few hours as Mark is examined and sent for some lab tests. Finally they take us out to eat, before dropping us off at home.

I find out that my vision is becoming blurry due to cataracts. I line up a driver for the day of my first operation, but then she comes down with Covid at the last minute. After I am done panicking I remember Mark's friend Chris, who has taken him fishing and been so good to him. I call Chris to see if he is willing to drive us and then keep Mark company during the hours of the operation. He consents willingly. Luckily Mark feels comfortable with Chris, and all goes well.

When I remember that I am "merely experiencing", reality shifts around me. What a "marvelous opportunity" to discover the kindness of people and to have it demonstrated to me that I am not alone.

24

Forgiveness

Mark's Story

My mother had multiple sclerosis. She expended so much energy trying to knock me out of the way of the car that she was reduced to a wheelchair. I was assigned to take care of her. Since I was making the meals, I could eat what I wanted, and they couldn't do anything about it. So I became a vegetarian. I was probably remembering all my lifetimes as a druid, as a monk in Tibet and others. It felt as if I were taking more charge of my life. That was also when I learned compassion.

The last time I saw my mother was when I was seventeen. We were both sitting in the living room. I was listening to some music that was very dark, some hard rock. My mother was watching me. I was singing along. She saw how unhappy I was at that moment and that I was ready to just chuck it all, leave this body. I didn't know how to escape the darkness. The darkness is not knowing the Love.

I went to the kitchen for a glass of water. When I came back, she looked at me and asked, "How can I get rid of this hatred?" She actually GOT it. I turned around and went back to the kitchen. I was shaking. My body wanted to hurt her, for all the hurt and torture she had put me through as a child.

But then I turned around and walked back to her and said, "The hatred that you've felt, that you've acted on in this life, LEAVE it in this life, leave it here."

Then she asked me to forgive her for how she'd treated me. I said, "I forgive you. Leave it all here." I had to decide on my own to forgive her, and I did. This is what freed *me*. I no longer felt like hurting her. I was freed of my own anger. I never saw her again. She died soon after.

I was still heavy into drugs, marijuana, LSD and others, but I no longer felt out of control. I was able to begin to really live my life. When someone who has injured you, tortured you even, asks forgiveness, and you are able to forgive them, then you are freed as well. I later stopped all drugs and have not touched any since I was around nineteen.

That was the beginning of me saving myself. But it never would have happened if I hadn't had my grandparents. They helped me by loving me and teaching me through Love—discipline with Love—and the way they taught me to communicate with and become one with Nature. The love that Nature gives us is always there with us. We only have to open to it.

25

Taking Its Toll

Phyllis' Journal

May 20, 2022: I have a meltdown. On the surface it's from frustration at not being able to find things I use every day, things I need in order to keep our lives functioning. Mark moves things, takes things, hides things and then has no memory of it. If I ask, "Where is (whatever)?" he doesn't know what I am talking about, he doesn't seem to recognize the word. He will shuffle over to a pile of stuff and start handing me things. He seems even more out of it lately. I talk to him as if he understands, and he'll respond by grunting, or he'll just say, "Yes, yes!" Most of the time I feel he doesn't understand anything, although now and then he seems to.

I watch online videos about what's happening in the world. When he watches with me, sometimes he seems interested, but maybe he's just focusing on trying to understand. He seems more engaged with spiritual videos and music.

This day I find myself escaping to the woods, sobbing for a long time. Leaning against a tall hemlock, unable to stop crying, I ask for help. I am holding on to my chest, folding in around the intense pain I am feeling.

The world around us is going crazy. Is it any wonder that I, too, succumb? Or that Mark feels the energy and acts out as well? I'm told, "Feel your feelings. Don't bury them. Otherwise they will take you over." So I breathe, I acknowledge the intense pain I feel about the world situation as well as watching my life partner slipping away, his mind less and less able to process current reality.

I go to the garden to check that the water to the hose is turned off. It got left on a few nights ago, dripping all night. Today I note that the little bean plants which had just poking been up out of the ground had been covered up by straw. I clean off the straw. The seedlings look pale and sick. I hope they survive. This is our food for the winter. I know it's useless to try to explain to Mark why he shouldn't cover plants in the garden. I just have to be more vigilant. Do I even have it in me to be more vigilant than I already am, or try to be? I decide to let go of the garden. Let him do as he likes. At least it keeps him occupied and in the yard.

Mark is up all night. We go to bed, but he is up again. And again, and again. Up and rummaging around the house. I try to sleep, but finally get up around 4 AM and manage to coax him back to bed. He is up around 7, acting even more confused than usual. I am already eating breakfast, so I serve him instead of going for his usual morning shower. He eats slowly. When I check the bathroom, I find his towel is wet. He must have managed some sort of shower in the wee hours of the night, while I was comatose with exhaustion. Perhaps he took a shower in his clothes?

He wanders outside while I clean up the dishes. I hear him shouting at invisible people. I go out to try to calm him down and notice he has no shoes on. I was too tired myself this morning to notice that. He is wandering around in his stocking feet, yelling angrily.

"I want you to die!" he shouts as he sees me. I respond calmly, "Well I will some time. Maybe sooner than not." I feel calm, the calm that sometimes settles on me beyond despair. Is this what they call surrender? Or am I just numb?

It takes a while, but eventually I am able to coax him to come inside to put on his shoes. He calms down. My mind knows he cannot help it. My heart grieves, wracked with unimaginable pain. He, too, is in pain. "I have nothing!" he often shouts. We go on. I keep trying to find some meaning in all of this. I struggle to find some meaning. I go on.

May 30-31: Mark is up again in the middle of the night. I go back to sleep. When I wake around 4 AM I go looking for him. He is scrunched up on a small love seat in the living room. I wake him and lead him back to bed. He seems confused.

July 5: I'm up around 4 AM to go to the bathroom. I don't notice Mark is not in bed. As I'm leaving the bathroom, the doorbell rings. It's Mark, outside in his stocking feet, very wet. There are very wet shoes sitting on the porch. Luckily it's not cold out. I have no idea how long he has been out there.

I know that much of Mark's rage and lashing out stems from a deep-seated fear. He doesn't understand what is happening to him. The world doesn't make sense, and that is frightening. It must be terrifying to awaken each day to a new and unknown environment.

This is probably why people with dementia often like routines. Sometimes they can grab onto a familiar pattern in their life, dredge up a forgotten memory that is strong because it has been so often repeated. And yet, in Mark's case at least, he also becomes bored, missing interaction with other people, even though he is no longer able to converse or even understand much of what they say. This boredom may be behind some of his restless nighttime roaming and daytime excursions.

26

My Druidic Education: Male/Female Balance and Rewiring the Brain

Mark's Story

My grandfather was born in 1893 and came to the US in 1902. He came alone, at age nine, from Prince Edward Island, because he had a brother waiting for him here. He was strong physically, mentally and spiritually, although he had very little formal education. A strong body was necessary to survive then. There were no machines or electricity to do the work, so you had to use your body.

His marriage to my grandmother was a partnership. My grandmother dealt with certain aspects of their life together, and my grandfather handled other aspects. Today, looking back, I see their division of labor as traditionally sex-oriented for the most part, although my grandmother worked as a caterer and brought in much of the income, while my grandfather farmed and took care of the land. But they were Druids, so they fully respected each other as equal partners, as much as was possible in the times they lived. Although they had their differences, and sometimes loud ones, there was always an underlying respect and kindness. They would never intentionally truly hurt one another, physically or psychically.

When my grandmother died at age 75, my grandfather couldn't figure out how to be here anymore. He had a stroke that cut off access to the left side of his body—the feminine side. They had truly had a partnership, two parts of a whole. Now he was missing his other half, literally.

When I visited him in the hospital, I told him, "I really need you around." I feel now that I should have let him go, but he loved me and understood that I wasn't yet ready to face the world alone. He told me, "I don't know if I can do it"-meaning stay here. But within 15 days he had put himself back together. He'd decided it was necessary to work with me for a while longer.

He didn't put it in terms of male and female energy. He just said he knew he was missing something. He reached out and asked his guidance, what he called "the angels", and they gave him pictures of what to do. Being who he was, he had the strength to be able to do what was necessary to repair his body and rewire his brain. The reason he could do that was that he had worked with my grandmother so long that he realized he could expand himself to access and develop the more feminine part of himself. He lived for another fifteen years.

I tell this story to let people know what is possible, what we are capable of doing. Yes, he was a Druid, and yes he had a strong body from his upbringing at the end of the 19th century. But he also would tell me that he was more dense than I was, because of when he was born. People today are even less dense. It is becoming easier and easier to access our multidimensional consciousness, our true capabilities. We have only to believe that we can do it and open to the energies that will help us to raise our vibrations.

And of course, live in love without conditions and without judgment, for ourselves and others.

Note from Phyllis: Mark told me that one time, when he was around nineteen years old, he was doing something spiritually that he should not have been doing. He felt he was hit by lightning. This may have been physical lightning or a flash in his brain, I don't know. At any rate, he realized it was a message from his higher Self. He lost use of his left brain for a while. He was able to reconstruct enough to continue his life, but he realized this was a spiritual wake up call. Later when his brain started deteriorating with dementia, he was no longer able to do this reconstruction. When he continually moaned, "I have nothing!" he may have been referring to a loss of conscious connection to his higher dimensional Self. Since he could not rebuild his brain this time, it must have been his time to leave.

27

It's Getting Scary

Phyllis' Journal

September 20, 2022: Mark is exhibiting uncontrolled laughter and uncontrolled sobbing, and he's showing more loss of recognition of simple objects.

December 1: I feel I am reaching a breaking point. I'm going along thinking I'm doing great, and then something happens, even something little, and I implode. I start crying. Of course this upsets Mark, who doesn't understand.

December 8: After two nights of being the energizer bunny, batteries running constantly, Mark finally slept last night. This morning he is frantic. He runs out into the snow in his socks, moaning, "I'm going to die!" He is extremely anxious for quite a while.

I'm feeling okay, nothing seems to bother me. Then suddenly I collapse, melt down, cry uncontrollably. I think I'm experiencing caretaker burnout.

December 17-18: Mark is up and down at night nine to ten times at least. I'm vacuuming this morning. I go to vacuum the hallway. Mark is there and yells at me. He never minded the vacuum before. Now he seems enraged at me. He comes at me. I back up. He pushes me. I trip over the vacuum cleaner and fall to the floor. I hit my right hip (the bad one) and twist to hit my left hand on the floor.

I yell back at him, "I can't live with you! I refuse to be a battered woman!" I am crying, shouting back. Later he denies it all, acts the martyr. "I didn't do anything to you." I was scared. I told him, "I can't trust you."

Mark is up and down all night. I give him some essence sleep drops. He finally comes to bed, but then I can't sleep. I stay up late reading. When Mark leaves the bed, he needs help getting covered when he comes back. Now that it's cold, there are layers of covers. I end up feeling exhausted after multiple times. I almost call his daughter, but I remember her calling the state police a few years ago, which led to months of hell with the judicial system. I'd like some help, some company. Also she says she doesn't know what to do with her dog if she comes to visit, since I am allergic to dog hair. And she works full time. So a visit probably won't happen.

December 19: I'm listening to "helpful tips" about dealing with stress, on a TV morning show.

"Breathe" they say. Okay, that's good.

"Get sleep". How do I do that, with a partner who is up and down all night and then needs help getting back in bed?

"Lessen stress". How? You obviously never lived with someone with dementia!

Now some woman is saying, "Listen". but how can I listen when he has no words, emotions I can't always understand: frustration certainly, rage and aggression.

"Have compassion". Well, I'm working on that all the time.

"Build inner resources". Sigh. Mine seem to be at a very low level. Used up? I'm lonely. I have no one to talk to when Mark goes off the rails.

Her advice: "Smile. Slow down. Mindfulness. Intention. Listen. Compassion. Take five. Begin with gratitude." Most of that seems like just words to me right now. I need some compassion for myself.

Now she says, "What is your vision of what you want?" I really don't know. I no longer can envision Mark being whole again. I no longer see a life for him or for me. I don't know how to do my "service" any more. I started reading David Wilcock's *Michael Prophesies*, which seem to offer a light at the end of the tunnel.

December 23: I decide to prepare for Christmas. Last year we didn't have Christmas at all, because Mark was so sick. I didn't feel well either. It wasn't "covid". Mark was shaking, had a fever. He was really out of it. Our herbalist friend says it sounds like a recurrence of Lymes, or some tick disease. Mark had tested positive for Anaplasmosis and Babesiosis, not Lymes, back in 2016, but sometimes you can have Lymes without knowing it, since the others can cover it up.

I don't know what I had. Maybe it was mild covid, or something else. Anyway I'm trying for a real Christmas this year. I will cook us a chicken and make squash pies.

December 30:

My Prayer for the New Year:
May I feel the joy of existence in all the little things.
May I be patient with Mark, and with myself.
Thank you for the beauty in my life.
May I be open to seeing and feeling it.
May I greet each morning with a smile,
And walk through each day with an open heart.
And may I be able to forgive myself when I can't.

January 1, 2023: Mark is up at 2:30 AM. He had peed in his pants. I help him shower and then into clean clothes. He is upset. I try to calm him down, telling him it isn't his fault. Both of us are very tired.

January 19: I take a caregiver burnout test at our caregiver Zoom meeting. A score of 40-60 means moderate to severe burnout. I got 51, which means I'm "doing too much." WTF? What can I STOP doing?

March 23: More and more Mark has been taking my things, moving them around, often losing them. I can no longer have stuff. "My" doesn't exist any more, and although I admire the Buddha, I don't feel totally there yet about having no possessions. Mark has gone off with my French Press. My cup of coffee in the morning is a sort of refuge for me from my situation as a caregiver. It's something I can look forward to and enjoy for at least a few moments every day. I feel that has been taken from me *too!* I finally figure out how to make coffee using a tea strainer—not rocket science. Why did I get so upset? I am learning to adapt. I make up with Mark, apologize for yelling at him, and we hug.

28

Adventures In Indian Country

Mark's Story

When I visited Hopi land with some friends, I met Grandfather David. He was then the oldest living Hopi. He had been blinded around 10 years earlier while chopping wood. He came out and sat down with us. All of a sudden Grandfather David turned into my grandfather. I blinked, and he changed back into Grandfather David again. Now he was smiling at me. He was looking right at me. The light coming out of his eyes was nailing me. He understood, by showing me my grandfather, who was an unusual man of his time for holding lovingness, that he saw me. David poured light into my body and smiled and smiled. Then I cleared my throat, and he turned to the others.

My friend Arthur was living around Hopi land. He told me

about when he was driving down a highway with Grandfather David and some other Hopi. Grandfather David decided he wanted some quiet. The car suddenly stopped. The other men in the car jumped out of the car to try to fix it.

A woman who was in the car turned to David and asked, "Grandfather, if you can just stop the car like that, why don't you fix all the craziness that's going on?"

He replied, "We could shut it down, but the strength of the people who are out of balance will just remake it. They don't understand the balance."

I went back to Cambridge to go to work, because I needed cash. It was 1978. I was twenty-nine. A friend called me from a gathering in Canada, saying, "Mark, we need you up here."

I said, "Bessie (my truck) isn't quite ready yet and I don't have blankets and food for a trip. I just put all my money into fixing Bessie."

She said, "Don't worry, just come here and we'll take care of you."

A few days later I was walking down a street in Cambridge when an Indian guy came up to me. "I hear you're going to Canada," he said. I hadn't told anyone about the phone call. "How're you going there?" he continued. I took him back and showed him Bessie. He gave me his name and phone number.

"We live in Roxbury," he said. Could you pick us up and take us with you?"

I told him, "Sure"

"My family's coming along as well," he added. I said that was okay with me. The place I was headed wasn't too far from where they were going.

When the time came to leave, he phoned me. I was just walking out the door. I picked them up in Roxbury. It was really cool. There was an elder lady, a grandmother, as well as a daughter, a 14 year old boy, and three young kids. The grandmother got into Bessie and looked around. She saw that there was a place to cook and everything, but it was all home-made. I could see she felt right at home. They all made themselves at home.

We drove way up in Canada. We got to the gathering where my friend was. She acted surprised to see me and asked why I was there. I told her she had promised to take care of me if I came up. She said, "I can't do that," and left me.

My passengers had paid me for the gas, but I hadn't thought beyond arriving there. The three women—grandmother, daughter and child—went into a huddle. They came out and said, "You come with us. You are meant to come with us. We will take care of you."

They took me to another gathering. I didn't realize at the time that there were representatives of over three hundred tribes gathering there, mostly medicine people, from South and Central America, Mexico, the US, and Canada.

As we drove in, the looks people were giving me were really hostile. The grandmother told me, "You'll be all right. Just keep going." Some relatives had saved them a place to camp. I looked around. There were *no* white people anywhere. I parked where they told me.

The grandmother said, "For this gathering we have gone to

great lengths *not* to have any white people here." The Native people were worried that the white people, with their atom bombs, would knock the earth off its axis. They wanted to figure out what kind of medicine energy they'd have to put into the ethers to stop this from happening. This was the purpose of that gathering.

The gathering lasted seven days. Every day people would come up to me and say, "You are special, and we want you to talk to us about what we can do." Broken Arrow was, of course, with me. But I couldn't stand up and talk to them. I didn't believe I could do what they wanted. One reason was the waves of anger and hatred that I felt directed towards me by many. There were people who told me that they wanted to kill me, but they didn't want to deal with the repercussions.

I spent almost all of my time at the sweat lodge, sweating and fire keeping. One day I drove my truck to bring back wood. I drove across a wet field, where I got stuck down to the axles. They got a tractor to pull me out, but it too got stuck. So then they got a bigger tractor to pull both vehicles out. They were pretty nice about it.

A medicine man, who was one hundred and five years old, told me, "If you'd come to us, we would have shown you where you could drive safely to get the wood." It was a slap. That helped me to begin to feel comfortable there.

When the gathering broke up, I took the family home to Roxbury. They paid my way. By the time I dropped them off, I felt like part of the family, as much as was possible, even though I never saw them again. I found out later that reporters wanted very badly to enter that gathering, to find out what was going on, but they hadn't been allowed in.

Mark and Bessie a few months before his transition.
Photo by Stephen Dallmus

29

Transition

Phyllis' Journal

March 27, 2023: As I am helping Mark get ready for his morning shower, he suddenly collapses. His eyes roll up into his head, and he falls to the floor, shaking uncontrollably. Luckily I am standing right by him, so I am able to ease his body down. He doesn't move or speak for a while. Then when he comes to, he tries to get up. I try to help him, but we can't manage to get his legs working. I call 911. So begins the nightmare of hospitals and medications.

The doctors want to figure out what has caused the blackout, so they attach diodes to his head. At the same time, they give him powerful anti-seizure medications. I wonder how they expect to note seizure-causing changes in his brain when he is on those meds, but that's what they do. He keeps trying to leave the bed at first. I know he is trying to get to the bathroom. They are afraid to let him up, so they medicate him until he looks like a zombie and can't go anywhere.

Finally they decide it wasn't a seizure, because they can't find any visible changes in his brain. I say, "Okay then, what do you call it when someone starts shaking uncontrollably and falls to the floor with his eyes going back into his head, blacks out and then can't get up?" They can't answer me. I guess they don't have a definition for that. If they can't find brain abnormalities that show up in their available scan machinery then it didn't happen? They finally decide it's just "progressing dementia" and they let us take him home.

Mark's daughter has come from Maine to help take care of him. I am very grateful. I'd hate to have him die in an institution. So would she.

Hospice sets up a bed in our living room. They are wonderful! A nurse comes once or twice a week and a bather comes every weekday. Mark deteriorates rapidly but holds on. Finally after around two weeks he stops eating and begins breathing with difficulty. It still takes him two days to let go.

The last night I am sitting by him, playing my guitar and singing to him. Then I lie down to rest a bit. Suddenly I become aware of a deep silence. The raspy breathing has stopped. I can tell he is gone.

A nurse comes an hour later to officially declare him dead, a little after midnight. Then around 3 AM the undertaker shows up. In my last image of Mark he is cocooned in a lovely dark red sheet being rolled out of the house on a gurney. The young man taking care of his body is very gentle and kind.

I call to leave a message for his daughter, who had gone home a few days earlier to take up her life again. I figured she would notify the rest of Mark's family. In the morning I call my family to let them know.

The next day I receive an email from one of our good friends, John Armitage, a metaphysical teacher who is currently in Europe. He says Mark had showed up and they had a two hour conversation about all their other lifetimes together. He says Mark is being well taken care of on the "other side", and he wants us to know that he is grateful for all the care that we had given him.

I hold a small memorial for Mark around a month later. I couldn't manage it before then. Some good friends come to stay with me and help out. I would have been lost without those friends, and I am very grateful. I wish they lived closer.

A tear's a drop of water
Leaking from the heart
Sorrow overflowing
Inside out

Carrying a message
To the soul:
"Please, until the pain is gone,
Help me not feel so alone."

Phyllis Brooks
February 8, 2021

30

When I Met Mark

Phyllis' Story

I remember the first time I met Mark. He was around thirty five. He was a little taller than me, slight of build, bushy curly dark hair and beard almost obscuring his downturned face. A bit shy, I thought. My son's father and I were moving into a house that needed a lot of work to be habitable, although the rent was right (free for taking care of it).

Mark was a carpenter. I had seen him at Dance Free in Boston a few times. He was an enthusiastic dancer, although a bit stiff. He seemed to limit himself to a square pattern on the dance floor, as if he didn't quite know how to let it all out. What I loved about the Dance New England dances I attended was the freedom to move all over the dance floor, body movements inspired by the music. I usually danced by myself, as did many others.

My partner at the time approached him about working on the house. We welcomed his help in making it habitable. Mark agreed to help fix up the house in exchange for having a room there, so he could escape the city on weekends.

When Mark came out to western Massachusetts, I took him to see the house in question. It was just twilight. He pulled back at first from entering the house, saying the energy felt dark. It felt kind of spooky to me as well in the semi-dark.

The house dated back to the late 1700's. We later found out that local legend spoke of a previous tenant (possibly the builder of the house) being somewhat unhinged. He would stand out on the road waving his penis at passing cars. It turned out he had lived there with his wife, his daughter, and his daughter by his daughter. He had died in the house.

This man's spirit was definitely hanging around. He would walk through us at times; it felt icky and cold, as if he was inhabiting all the spaces between my molecules, making me feel twice as heavy as normal. He started appearing in my dreams, making sexual advances. This was when we decided he had to go.

Mark and I held a ceremony to send him on his way. We called in angels to lead him to the Light. He said "All I wanted was love."

My then partner, the father of my two-year-old son, was often gone, driving cross-country for the Green Tortoise, a hippie bus company. I would receive postcards from his various sexual encounters across the country. They were not subtle. Mark could see that I was not being treated well, and that I was unhappy. It bothered him.

One night as I lay in bed by myself as usual, I felt Mark in my head. He was sleeping in his van, out in the yard, since the room he was creating for himself was not yet ready. I answered him with my thoughts and then went out to him. He said he didn't know anyone else he could speak mind-to-mind with like that. I was better at receiving than sending. It felt wonderful to be that close with someone. He felt a connection with me from other lifetimes together. I felt a connection, although I was not as good at remembering details of other lifetimes.

I was pretty much a single mom. My son was two when Mark moved in. I had not had a break from motherhood since his birth. My son was around three when I wanted to attend a sound healing workshop over a weekend. Mark volunteered to take care of him.

When I got back, my son was excited about his adventures with Mark over the weekend. "For breakfast he got a big bowl and poured a whole box of cereal into it. Then he poured in milk and got out two spoons and we ate it together!" That was Mark, unconventional and inventive. He did what he wanted when he wanted and listened to his own drummer.

Soon after that Mark left on a cross-country trip. Being a carpenter, he could find work wherever he went. He especially liked to visit the southwest and Hopi country. He would phone us now and then. I'm not usually a phone person, but I could talk with Mark for an hour or more.

I didn't feel right about leaving my son's father, even though he was hardly ever there and was having sexual relations with women all over the country on his bus trips. When I confronted him about the postcards from his various lovers, he responded, "I don't like to sleep alone."

Still, when he found out that I was seeing Mark in his absence, he went ballistic. A true double standard. When they were both around, the atmosphere in the house became very tense. I'm sure it contributed to the fire that broke out in the chimney that went through Mark's room above the kitchen. It burned his room and possessions first. Then the entire house was compromised. The local fire department did their best, but it was December, and the water nearby was frozen. They only had what they could carry in their truck.

Both my sexual partners were adept at multidimensional energy manipulation ("magic" if you will). But my son's father had leaned towards the dark side in another lifetime and had a small army (nine) of nasty other dimensional beings at his beck and call, that he had conjured in an Atlantean lifetime. They worked for him, but they also often played tricks on him and worked against him. He was no longer consciously in control of them. They would do the bidding of his subconscious. They had put me into the hospital at least twice. Until I lived with him, I had no idea that such entities existed.

After the fire, Mark went traveling again. My son's father and I and our son moved into a nearby cabin. Then he took off again. I was left with a small child and a flock of ducks to take care of. The well to the cabin failed and I had to cart in gallons of water each day to keep the ducks alive—and wash out diapers. I didn't see much of Mark for a while, while he was traveling and then building his house.

One afternoon when my son was around six or seven and was away at school, his father was there in the cabin with me. He picked up a cast iron frying pan and came at me, yelling, "They want me to kill you!" With one hand he was waving the frying pan at me, with the other he was trying to hold back that arm. He had been hearing voices in his head that told him "they" wanted blood sacrifices. He told me he had been trapping rabbits in the woods and sacrificing them to the voices. Now they wanted human prey. They also wanted him to kill our son.

I fended him off (his heart wasn't into killing me or our son) and called a friend to come help. She showed up and chanted some Tibetan exorcism which seemed to calm him down. But after that I knew I had to escape with my son.

I didn't start living with Mark until a few years later. He was finishing building his house, and we moved in with him. I was with him for thirty years.

In 2016 I went away to a conference. He had been invited but declined. He felt he needed to stay and work. During the week and a half I was away he got bitten by two ticks while visiting a potential client. He became ill. He didn't let me know how ill he was when I phoned him every day. When I got back, he had lost coherent speech. His hearing was already bad. Gradually he also lost coherent thought.

The last seven years were difficult as he declined more and more. The entries from my caretaker's journal reflect those times, especially the last few years. I was glad to be able to keep him at home during his final days, so he could die in the house he had built on the land that he loved. I still miss him terribly.

31

Make Sure There Is A Will!

Phyllis' Journal

For a couple of years I had been attending a dementia caregiver's group on Zoom, sponsored by LifePath. We had been able to help each other a lot. They helped me to not feel so alone. We were able to tell each other what we were feeling, give each other tips on various behaviors, and advise each other on how to keep (relatively) sane (and what to do when we couldn't). No one who has not cared for someone with dementia can possibly understand the toll it takes. I remember once someone telling me, "You are doing such a good job with him! It must be really hard." I answered, "It's harder for him." But yes, it was difficult for me as well.

People in grief can act unpredictably and irrationally. A man in the dementia caregiver Zoom group was taking care of his ailing mother. He became very upset at the treatment he was receiving from the rest of his family. They had advice for him on how he should be doing things, but they did not come to help him. They were very critical of everything he was doing. He realized that they probably felt guilty for not being there and were projecting it onto him to avoid facing their own grief. They resented that he was doing what they should have been helping to do. It frustrated and hurt him. Then when his mother died, these relatives came like vultures to take what they wanted of hers. I remember thinking, "I'm glad I have a good relationship with Mark's family. That would never happen to me."

Never say never. By the time Mark is ready for discharge from the hospital, I am a basket case. I'd been taking care of him by myself for seven years. Lately this included driving to the hospital every day for over two weeks, an hour each way. On this last day I am sobbing almost uncontrollably, knowing that I am on my way to take him home to die. I almost can't drive.

I arrive at the hospital expecting his daughter to be there as promised, but she isn't. After a few hours I call to find out where she is and to tell her I need her. I want someone to lean on. She is stuck in traffic and resents me being all bent out of shape that she isn't there yet. I guess she had hoped to be able to lean on me. Neither of us is capable of supporting anyone at that point, not even ourselves.

We'd always gotten along very well in the past. Mark and I had gone to Maine to help her when she was finishing up the house Mark and her mother had bequeathed to her. Then when a tenant had trashed the place, we went again to help clean it up. We went a few other times, mostly building related, and once for a week or so to take care of her after an operation. She had come down to help clean up our place so we could achieve propane coverage, and she had come on visits now and then. I really loved her, and she acted as if she loved me back.

Now I welcome her and her dog, in spite of my allergies. It's a sweet dog. I'll make do. Relations between us continue to worsen. We don't always agree on how to take care of Mark. I usually go along with her eventually, in order to keep the peace.

I find out later she had told my son that I had said things to her I never said (or even thought), and she had twisted things I had said.

She misses her life in Maine and begins to resent the time she is spending here. Seeing how much her father has deteriorated in the four years since she had last seen him, and watching him slowly die, proves difficult for her. It is difficult for me as well, although I have watched the deterioration happen gradually. At one point she threatens to truck Mark off to Maine. This is totally irrational. Even in the unlikely event that he could make the journey, she would have to hire caregivers while she resumed her work. Luckily Mark had managed a few years earlier to sign a health care proxy, making me his primary caregiver, so he remains at home.

Why is Mark's daughter so angry with me? She does a great job cleaning up the yard, supposedly to help me after Mark's death. She buys me presents, whether or not I need or want them. Then she talks to me as if I am dirt on her shoe. When two of my friends drive a long way to support me emotionally and say goodbye to Mark, his daughter seems uncomfortable. Until now only Mark's family has visited. I begin to realize how much she needs to feel in control.

One friend has just taken a course on healing with crystals. She mentions that she is looking for six small crystals to make mandalas.

I ask if she'd like some of Mark's many crystals, in order to remember him. She agrees, and we all go to look at them. Mark's daughter enters the room, obviously extremely distressed and shaking uncontrollably.

"This doesn't feel right to me!" she cries. "We should have discussed it first!" Well, I was under the impression that we had done just that the day before and agreed to try to sell some online. But in the face of her distress, I and my friends stop and leave the room. Later I tell Mark's daughter she can have all the crystals, except a few that were mine. Arguing over Mark's crystals seems unconscionable. I hope their energy helps her in her grief.

She packs up her truck with all Mark's usable tools and leaves, two days before he dies. A week later she shows up to take all the crystals.

Mark and I had never been formally married. He also never made a will. As a blood relative, his daughter has a legal right to dispose of Mark's ashes after the cremation. She decides to have them sent to her in Maine. When I find out about the ashes, my only consolation is that's she must be really hurting to be so vindictive. Is she trying to erase me from his life?

Mark's daughter left her life and work temporarily in order to come help take care of Mark, so that he could die in his own home. She has spent a lot while here, on supplies to help us take care of Mark, on caretakers when she couldn't be in the house, and on gas, driving back and forth to Maine. Previously I had gotten her listed as the beneficiary on Mark's small life insurance policy,.This was to reimburse what she had spent already as well as to pay her for repairs she planned to make on Mark's house. She was going to be repaid and more.

So, the man in the dementia caregiver Zoom group was right. People in grief can act irrationally and unpredictably. You never know how they will react to their loved one's death, or what they may take out on the caregiver. It helps me a little to have heard his story. I try not to blame Mark's daughter too much and focus on all that she did for him. She was grieving, just as I was. I only wish we could have grieved together, in love, instead of the way it turned out.

32

Previous Life and Other Lifetimes

Mark's Story

I hadn't written down Mark's narration of his life story between the time of his grandfather's death and when I met him, except for his adventures in Indian country. He did tell me some of the rest however.

Mark had used a lot of drugs from age twelve onwards. The father of one of his friends worked where he had access to LSD. Mark was also into pot, speed, alcohol, heroin and whatever would keep the voices of others out of his head and help him forget or deal with his memories of abuse. He may have forgiven his mother just before her death, but he still carried the heavy emotional burden of what she had done to him. Also he could hear other people's thoughts.

At some time during his college years he'd had a revelation. He said he was hit by lightning. He felt his higher self was after him to clean up his act, so he quit all drugs, cold turkey. Mark's way of managing this incredible challenge was by sitting for days, looking out of his window, watching a bud on a tree slowly open into a flower. His early connection with Nature was reactivated. At the end of this ordeal he was seeing everything surrounded by a violet light, and he felt renewed.

Mark had worked briefly at some company in the Boston area after he had graduated college with an accountant degree, but when his boss told him to start keeping two sets of books, he refused. He left and started working in construction.

Mark lived for a time with a woman in Maine, and they had a daughter. Then when this woman went back to her old boyfriend, Mark left Maine. He found Maine to be a very parochial state. Not being from there made it difficult to find work.

Mark met his second partner at a festival. He had been at Woodstock, but I don't know if it was there or elsewhere. They also had a daughter. His multidimensional Team told him this was necessary, because that soul needed to incarnate right away or it would regress in its development. His Team also promised that he would be taken care of afterwards.

This second partner would beat on him. Because of his memories of his mother's abuse, he had a hard time not responding. He finally left her so he wouldn't lose his temper and hurt her back. She was from a wealthy family so would be taken care of. Then he wandered around the country in his truck, Bessie, mostly in the southwest, when he wasn't working in the Boston area in construction.

He remembered many of his previous lifetimes. He had been a monk in Tibet, a counselor of some kind in China, and a Druid in ancient Britain. In 2000 we travelled to England to attend a Wesak ceremony being held in Glastonbury by our friend and teacher, John Armitage. Wesak celebrates the birthday of the Buddha. Being in Glastonbury brought up memories for Mark of his Druid lifetimes.

We climbed up Glastonbury Tor. Looking out over the landscape to the west, Mark could see in his memory a swampland, during a time when Glastonbury had been an island. A boat was approaching with two boys in it, coming to learn what the Druids had to teach them. It was Jesus and Luke, twelve and fourteen years old, brought by Jesus' uncle Joseph of Arimathea. Joseph was a trader in tin who often travelled to Britain. The young Jesus later travelled to Egypt and India as well for training before beginning his Palestinian ministry. Mark remembered meeting the boat and being one of the teachers for the two boys. John Armitage had been Luke in that lifetime. They had fun reminiscing. Both had been in service to this planet for a long time. Now they were continuing that service.

The day after Mark's transition, I received an email from John. He'd just had a long conversation with Mark, mostly about their other shared lifetimes. He assured me that Mark was being well cared for and appreciated the care we'd given him before his passing.

Many times Mark had been a Scout in Native American lifetimes. A Scout was a spiritual occupation which involved protecting the tribe. His major spiritual guide this time around was called Broken Arrow. They had been brothers in some of his Native lifetimes. Eventually he found out that Broken Arrow was an aspect of Thoth, the Egyptian guardian. In this current life Mark had had encounters with extra-terrestrials who were here to help with the ascension of the planet, just as he was. This was all commonplace for him. He also told me he and I had had numerous lifetimes together in varying roles: as partners, father-daughter etc., since we were from the same soul family.

He seemed ready to settle down when he built his own house. Eventually I moved in with him and lived there for 30 years.

The house that Mark built.

33

Consequences for Caregivers

Phyllis' Journal

Caregivers live under stress day and night. They experience constant verbal and energetic abuse from their loved one, and sometimes also from the extended family. It can take a toll.

Soon after Mark's memorial I start feeling intense pain, at first in my head and then around my waist. I find out I have a growth on one of my kidneys. The urologist wants to take out the kidney. I figure he knows what he is doing, so four months after Mark died, I end up in the hospital. "The operation went well," says the surgeon, although he seems bemused that "there wasn't much blood".

A week and a half later we find out where the blood has gone. I wake with pain in my left leg. It is swollen to twice the size of the other. Immediately I suspect a blood clot. The on-call person for the urology clinic (it was on a weekend) admonishes me to go immediately to the emergency room. Luckily a friend has been staying with me to help my recovery, so she drives me to the hospital.

The next day I undergo another operation, this time to clear out the clot from my blood vessel, from my knee to my heart area, and have a stent put in to keep it open. This surgeon prescribes a blood thinner (Eliquis). When I go to pick it up at the pharmacy, I find that it costs over $200 for a four- day supply, and after that I have to fork over $500 for a two- week supply. The doctor wants me to take this blood thinner for six months, but I cannot afford it. My local clinic helps me find a less expensive medication. Unfortunately this one (Warfarin) listed the following cautions:

> **You may have a higher risk of serious bleeding if you:**
>
> - **are 65 or older**
> - **have had trauma such as...surgery**
> - **have [had] kidney problems**
> - **take other medications that increase your risk of bleeding, including heparin.**

I am *seventy seven* at the time. I have just had *kidney surgery*. They had given me *heparin shots* while I was in the hospital. Nevertheless my healthcare providers forcefully recommended me to take this medication for six months *to prevent internal bleeding*.

A week later I when I wake up, I am peeing blood. It is a *lot* of blood. I am nauseous and experience a few full body convulsions, which are terrifying. I stop taking the blood thinner immediately and call the urology clinic for advice. They tell me to come in for a urinalysis two days later (again, it is a weekend). By then my urine looks like a grainy cup of black coffee, and I am in a lot of pain. It feels like a kidney infection to me. I have had them before but not for over forty years. Since I now have only one kidney left, this is problematic.

The urology clinic doctor prescribes an antibiotic. It is a terrible medication with many really awful possible side effects. The literature that comes with it warns not to use it *unless there is no alternative medication.* It is contra-indicated *for any kidney problems* and for *people over sixty*, among other things. This text was in boldface:

> **Ciprofloxacin tablets, a fluoroquinolone antibacterial medicine, can cause serious side effects. Some of these serious side effects can happen at the same time and could result in death.**

I refuse to take it and rely on lots of vitamin C and colloidal silver. By the end of the week I take in another urine sample that looks clear. The clinic calls the next day to say there are a few specks of blood still, and they prescribe another antibiotic, one that doesn't have such traumatic side effects. I decide to take this medication only if the pain comes back and my latest urinalysis still shows infection. My digestive system had been majorly disrupted by the surgeries and is just now coming back on line. Antibiotics would send me back to square one there. The urology clinic never calls me with the urinalysis results, so I have to assume it was clear.

Gradually my body replaces the lost blood, and I begin to feel better about being alive—something I continue to work on. The consequences of seven years of caregiving and loss are not easy to shed. I still tear up when someone who hasn't heard about Mark's death asks, "How is Mark?" Now I am becoming used to living by myself. Mark is better off being out of that damaged body. I figure he had accomplished his mission and was ready to go. Why he had to go that way, I do not know, may never know. It just was and is.

WHERE E'RE I GO

Where e're I go
There I am
Where e're I go
Here I am
Don't ask where
Don't ask when
Don't ask how
Or to what end
And especially
Especially
Especially don't ask WHY.

Phyllis Brooks
September 2022

34

Clearing and Closure

Phyllis' Journal

Just before the new year of 2024 my friend, Gwen, offers me help in exorcising some distressing mind loops that had been keeping me awake at night. I had been having trouble dismissing these thoughts that led me to re-experience acrimonious exchanges and energies with Mark's daughter and with my son. His daughter had made up and contorted things I had said which my son seemed to believe. All of it didn't make sense to me. I had never said the things she "repeated" from me. She also twisted things we had talked about. For instance, after visiting Mark in the hospital I commented that I'd rather he died than lived medicated into a zombie. That was no way to live. I knew that he would not want to exist like that, and I said neither would I. Later she said that I had threatened to kill Mark and myself!

Every time I tried to talk with her and clear things up, she would accuse me of "gaslighting" her. She seemed convinced she had heard me say things that I had not even thought, let alone said. My son also had told me that I was constantly criticizing him. I didn't even think critical thoughts about him, let alone utter any. All this was very confusing, but there was nothing I could do or say to change their attitude. Since I love them both, I was finding these recurring mind loops and their continuing antagonism extremely painful.

Gwen offers me a healing session with Chang, a lovely being she has been channeling recently. Chang has been a major multi-dimensional companion of our teacher, John Armitage, since his childhood. John later found out that Chang was a Chinese philosopher and Light being better known as Lao Tzu. I trust Chang and I trust Gwen's ability to accurately channel him, so I gratefully accept this healing session.

Chang brings through some flower and gem frequencies into my body and integrates them to clear me. He banishes some nasty fourth-dimensional entities that had been infesting Mark's daughter and my son in order to encourage their hateful thoughts about me. These beings would amplify the energy of the thoughts and direct them at me. Thoughts are energy. Such directed and enhanced thoughts were behind my recent physical challenges. In this way these entities hoped to dim my spiritual Light.

Chang banishes these entities from around me, from the land, from Mark's daughter and from my son. He affirms that these were the beings that my son's father had conjured during an Atlantean lifetime. They are now also cleared from their conjuror—my son's father—as well. They can no longer harm anyone.

I now wonder if these entities were tormenting Mark when he

was shouting at "invisible" beings to "get out of here!" Were they behind some of Mark's paranoid thoughts and actions as well?

Chang tells me that I am now clear and will heal completely. He encourages me to be happy and spread my light. I thank him and Gwen profusely. I ask Chang to greet Mark for me, and John Armitage as well. I know he can communicate easily with both. He tells me that Mark is always around me, as are many loving beings, ready to help me. I feel much lighter now.

WHERE I REST

I touch my heart, breathe slowly and deeply,
Let my consciousness drift
To around my heart
Becoming one with my inner flame.

Here a lotus
Envelopes me in soft petals
Of divine scent.

Quan Yin is here
Holding the tears of the world in her hands.
I am the tears
I am the hands.
Here I rest
A bright white light
Floating in velvet darkness.

Fears and anxieties
Fade into shadows,
Dissipate into nothingness.
Compassion floods my being.
I am everything
I am no thing
Here I rest.

Phyllis Brooks / June 20, 2021

Afterword

Advice to Caretakers

At the beginning I mentioned that my purpose was not to create another "how to" for caregivers of people with dementia. There are plenty of books and online videos about that. However I do wish to share here with fellow caregivers some things that helped me through the ordeal of taking care of a loved one who is experiencing progressive dementia.

I hope that you can relate to some of my experiences, both those where I did not fare so well and those that seemed to help. Often emotions would pile up inside me, frustration, pain, anger, despair. These needed to be released if I was to be able to continue my caregiving.

One powerful way that I found to release and be able to come back to my calmer self was to go out into Nature and be surrounded by the innate love manifested in creation. I reiterate that crying and screaming are great ways to let go of pent-up energies, as long as you remember to *breathe deeply* while you emote. Of course don't do this where your person can hear you! Mark used to say that the calm auras of the trees comb out our own energy fields as we walk among them. When I allowed it, this proved true.

Another aid I had in my home was a large sign:

**LOVE
IS ALWAYS THE ANSWER
NO CONDITIONS
NO JUDGMENTS**

This reminder in my face was invaluable when I felt myself teetering on the edge of sanity.

Most of us go into this dementia caregiving without any experience or idea of what it will involve. Usually as well the difficulties and challenges creep up on us as our person's behavior degenerates. The "experts" in the online videos and workshops are very helpful up to a point. I don't mean to devalue their input.

Often when I heard in online classes on caregiving, or from counselors advice on "how to deal with dementia", I would feel anger or frustration at the matter of fact admonishments. I resented their calm assumption that I *could* do all these things, and that they would work. Many of course did help, when I could apply them. Here I speak to fellow caregivers: *don't let anyone make you feel guilty or inadequate for not always being able to be one of their perfect caregivers.* **In my view, a perfect caregiver is one who loves enough to *be there* through it all, and who tries their best to continue to love and take care of their loved one, *and themself.* So there!** (Keep your sense of humor!)

Some connections I found useful were local elder services groups. Check your area for these.

And yes, many of those online or in person workshops on dementia can be helpful, even if you find yourself yelling at the screen. Just remember to *breathe* while you do it! Remember the above caveat about not feeling guilty or inadequate or taking any of their advice as gospel. Each person is different. You try things, and if they work, fine; if they don't, don't worry about it. Just try something else next time.

I also found any creative outlet to be invaluable. My writing group encouraged me to produce something at least every other week. Once I got that pen in hand, words would flow, emotions would be expressed, and I would feel better. Writing this book after the fact also helped me, especially in remembering the Mark I knew and relating some of his history. Other creative outlets for me were playing my guitar and baking. Whatever you enjoy doing will help.

Some physical things can help with stress. A healthy diet is important for you both. Organic food is essential for optimum health in our poisoned environment. Mark insisted on making organic vegetable juice every day that I knew him; this I continued throughout his dementia as well. Avoid products with glyphosate especially which includes most flours and products made with them. Do your research.

Electromagnetic pollution is ubiquitous. Mark and I used to sit on a couch in our living room to watch movies on TV. He started getting nosebleeds at the same time I started having really bad headaches. I found out about a process called Focused Life-Force Energy (FLFE.net) and tried a free trial subscription for fifteen days. From my work with flower essences and gem elixirs I knew the power of frequencies, so I was intrigued. Immediately Mark's nosebleeds and my headaches stopped. Apparently our electric meter had recently been changed to a "smart meter". It is attached to our house right on the other side of the wall behind our living room couch. Hmmm. Again, do your research. There are quite a few products out there with varying degrees of effectiveness.

For the rest of you who are not caregivers but have read this far: please, if you know someone with dementia, go to visit and communicate as best you can with them. Offer to stay an hour or two with the person so their caregiver can have some alone time. Keep in touch with them both. Caregiving can be a very lonely occupation, as can being a person experiencing creeping dementia.

Thank you for listening. I leave you in love,
Phyllis

Acknowledgements

This book would never have been written without the encouragement of my Woman Soul writing group. I thank also the people at LifePath who gave dementia caretaking workshops and encouraged us to keep a journal. It was difficult to do but helped me see patterns of behavior in Mark and to express my emotions, as well as just living them in the moment. Especially I thank Hazel Dawkins, author and longtime friend, for her willingness to read my manuscript and who offered invaluable advice.

My heartfelt thanks also goes to the compassionate ones who reached out to help Mark and myself. These include Chris Smith, who took Mark fishing, and who drove us to my medical appointments, keeping Mark company while I was there. Stephen Dallmus, who donated an afternoon a week to take Mark on walks, and who became good friends with both of us. The Wendell Council on Aging that supplied medical equipment free of charge. Love to all my friends in New Paradigm Multidimensional Transformation, especially John Armitage, who continued to send healing energy to Mark and then to me.

I thank my personal friends Diane Spindler Lucy Brewster, Barbara Allen, Ginny Rockwood and Yuk Yee Li-Downs who were willing to travel to come support me after Mark's passing and during my health challenges. Gwen Hunt and Alison Ali donated energy work. My former students, Beebe Mor, Landsie Jean and John O'Connell drove Mark and myself to a neurology appointment and visited us at home to provide company. My two sisters encouraged me from a distance as I navigated the healthcare system. I also appreciate the help that my son and Mark's daughter gave us.

Blessings on all of you!

Phyllis Brooks has been making & distributing flower & gem remedies since 1984. She teaches New Paradigm Multi-Dimensional Transformation, a self-empowerment modality. She is also an artist and a practitioner of Soul Wisdom remote energy clearings. She lives in western Massachusetts.

To hear the music that goes with some of the songs go to phyllismichal-brooks.com . Comments from caregivers welcome there as well!

Also by Phyllis M. Brooks: *Living in Freedom & Love Without Conditions: New Paradigm Multi-Dimensional Transformation* (Balboa Press)